6.45
SJ 11/07

Revise Modern World History

for OCR Specification 1937

Greg Lacey

Heinemann

Heinemann Educational Publishers
Halley Court, Jordan Hill, Oxford OX2 8EJ
Part of Harcourt Education

Heinemann is the registered trademark of
Harcourt Education Limited

First published 2002

10-digit ISBN: 0 435308 34 3
13-digit ISBN: 978 0 435308 34 6

09 08 07
10 9 8 7 6 5

Designed, illustrated and typeset by Tech Set Ltd, Gateshead

Printed and bound in UK by Bath Press

Picture research by Liz Moore

Photographic acknowledgements
The authors and publisher would like to thank the following for permission to
reproduce photographs:
AKG: 93 (bottom); Centre for the Study of Cartoon and Caricature/University of
Kent/Strube/Daily Express: 12; Centre for the Study of Cartoon and
Caricature/University of Kent/David Low/Evening Standard: 21; Conservative
Research Department: 61; David King: 121; Imperial War Museum: 75; Mary Evans
Picture Library: 68; Peter Newark's American Pictures: 154; Punch: 54, 122, 153;
Solo Syndication: 45

Cover photograph: © Hulton Getty

Contents

Introduction

What do I study in OCR Modern World History specification 1937?

The OCR Modern World History GCSE course consists of two compulsory topics and a range of optional Depth Studies, of which one must be studied for the written examination and either one or two for coursework. The compulsory topics are the Core Content, which covers *International Relations 1919–c.1989*, and the British Depth Study on *How was British society changed, 1906–18?* The optional Depth Studies offered in the written examination are *Germany 1919–45, Russia 1905–41, The USA 1919–41* and *China 1945–c.1976* (of these only Germany, Russia and the USA are covered in this book).

Here is a summary of the examination requirements:

OCR

Paper 1: 2 hours

This paper contains questions on the Core Content, and on the optional Depth Study you have chosen. It carries 75 marks (worth 45 per cent of the total assessment).

There are three sections.

In *Section A* you will have to answer **one** question from a choice of two on the Core Content. Each question will be source-based, and will have two parts. These questions will carry 15 marks each.

In *Section B* there will be four structured questions on the Core Content, of which you must answer **one**. Each question will have three parts and will carry 20 marks.

In *Section C* you have to answer a compulsory source-based question, which will have three parts and will carry 20 marks. You must also answer **one** structured question from a choice of two. Each of the structured questions will have three parts and will carry 20 marks. All questions in Section C are on the optional Depth Study you have chosen.

Paper 2: 1 hour 30 minutes

This paper is a source-based investigation of an issue taken from the British Depth Study. There will be between five and seven questions on the sources. All questions are compulsory. The paper carries 50 marks (worth 30 per cent of the total assessment).

Coursework

You will do two coursework assignments. These will be on either one or two of the optional Depth Studies. You cannot do coursework on the Depth Study you have chosen for the written examination. Coursework carries 50 marks (worth 25 per cent of the total assessment).

What sort of questions will I get?

In the examination, you will earn marks by showing the following skills:

Objective 1 – using your knowledge to describe, analyse and explain the events you have studied.

Objective 2 – using historical sources.

Objective 3 – demonstrating that you understand how and why the events you have studied have been interpreted and represented in different ways.

Objectives 2 and 3 will be tested in source-based questions (though using your knowledge to help you answer these questions, which counts as Objective 1, will also gain you marks). Objective 1 will be tested in structured questions.

What is in this revision guide?

We have covered the topics that most people will study for the written examination. These are:

International Relations 1919–c.1989 (including the origins of the Second World War and the development of the Cold War)

British Depth Study: How was British society changed, 1906–18? (including the reforms of the Liberal governments, the Suffragettes, and the impact of the First World War on British society)

Optional Depth Study: Germany 1919–45 (including the Weimar Republic, how the Nazis gained support and what it was like in Nazi Germany)

Optional Depth Study: Russia 1905–41 (including the overthrow of the Tsar, the Bolshevik takeover, and the regime of Stalin)

Optional Depth Study: The USA 1919–41 (including the boom of the 1920s, the impact of the Wall Street Crash, and the New Deal)

In each section you will find:

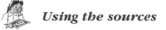

Topic summary

Sometimes studying History in depth can be confusing because you get to know so much detail that you lose sight of the 'bigger picture'. So we start each section with a summary of what the topic is about.

What do I need to know?

The revision guide then gives you a summary of what you need to know for the exam. Summary boxes are also included to give you a handy visual summary. When you have completed your revision you should be able to take a summary box and write at length about each point that is shown in it.

Key topics

Here we give you the basic facts about the topic, but not in the same kind of detail as in your textbook and notes. We are not telling you the whole story again, but instead are summarising it to make it easier for you to learn.

What do I know?

Once you have completed your revision you might like to test yourself to see how much you know. We have included a short self-assessment section so that you can see just how thorough your revision has been. Most of the questions can be answered from information given on the topic, but we also presume that you have been learning the information in your book and notes!

Using the sources

A vital part of the OCR Modern World History examination is being able to use sources. We have, therefore, included a number of 'using the sources' exercises in the book, which are matched with the types of source-based questions found in the different sections of the question papers. Sometimes we give you even more help by adding hints on how to answer the questions.

Exam type questions

You may just be studying History because you love it, and not be worried at all about the examination. For most students, however, what they really want is to do as well as possible in the examination. So we have given you lots of examples of the types of questions you will be asked, together with some student answers.

Examiner's comments

The author of this book is an experienced senior GCSE examiner, and has commented on each exam question answer. By reading the comments you will be able to see what is good and what is disappointing in the answer. Then you can make sure that any answer you give in the exam is much better.

What is the best way to revise?

1 Be organised
You can't revise properly if you don't have all the necessary material. So make sure that your work is in order and up to date.

2 Revise regularly
Revision is not something that you should leave until the last few weeks (or days!) before an exam. If you can learn as you go along, it will be much easier to take in everything before the final exam. Try to find a few minutes each week to go over what you have studied. If there is anything you haven't understood, get it cleared up straight away!

3 Plan a proper revision timetable
The last few months of your course can be a busy and worrying time, so make a sensible revision timetable and stick to it. Make sure you have set yourself realistic targets. You are the best person to judge exactly how much you can do in the time available. It's no good saying you will do eight hours' revision on a certain day, then fail to do it and get depressed. Much better would be to plan to do four slots of an hour each, with time between to relax and do something more enjoyable. Everyone's concentration lapses as time goes on, so the golden rule for revision should be little and often rather than forcing yourself to study for hours on end.

4 Use your guide
If you try to revise by simply reading your work, you are liable to get bored and you won't take it all in. So read a small section in your file, then turn to the relevant topic and make a few revision notes. Read these through and when you think that you know the material, try extending the points you have made. Once you are happy with the topic, answer the 'What do I know?' questions, and do the source and examination questions. After all that, you should be well prepared!

5 Stay cool
At examination time everyone feels under pressure. To do well you not only have to be properly prepared, but you also have to know how to stay relaxed. Resting is as important as working, so make sure you get a good night's sleep before each exam. Don't take any notice of what other people say about how much work they have (or haven't!) done. Stick to your own revision timetable and practise answering questions. Then you'll be fine, but make sure you arrive for the examination in plenty of time. You have enough to cope with without worrying about being late.

6 Be lucky
Lucky people get questions in the examination on the very bits they have revised most thoroughly, but the best approach is to make your own luck – revise properly and no matter what questions come up, you'll do well.

Here's hoping the revision goes well, the exam goes even better, and the results go best of all!

1 International relations 1919–c.1989

1.1 Were the peace treaties of 1919–23 fair?

Topic Summary

At the end of the First World War, Germany and the other defeated nations were forced to sign peace treaties with the victorious Allies. The French, in particular, wanted to make sure that Germany would never again be strong enough to threaten war. The terms of these treaties, and particularly those of the Treaty of Versailles, were seen by many, even at the time, as harsh and unfair.

What do I Need to Know?

You will need to understand what the Allies wished to achieve in the peace treaties, and why. You should know the terms of the peace treaties, and consider the impact of these terms both on the defeated nations and on Europe as a whole, with a particular emphasis on what happened in Germany up to 1923. This will enable you to judge for yourself whether or not the treaties were fair.

Key Topics

Background to the peace treaties

- In January 1919 delegates from 32 countries met in Paris to make peace.
- Europe was shattered by the First World War. Its economy was in ruins.
- Over 15 million people had been killed in the war.
- The Russian and Austrian empires had collapsed. A Bolshevik regime had been set up in Russia.
- The map of Europe had to be redrawn. Many nationalities wanted 'self-determination'.

What were the motives and aims of the 'Big Three' at Versailles?

- The 'Big Three' were Wilson (USA), Lloyd George (Britain) and Clemenceau (France). With the addition of Orlando (Italy), they are sometimes referred to as the 'Big Four'.

- In January 1918 Wilson issued his 'Fourteen Points'. He wanted these to be the basis for peace. However, at Versailles he was forced to compromise as other nations were less idealistic. He was weakened by lack of support back home. In 1920 the US Senate refused to ratify the treaties.
- Clemenceau wanted France to be secure from future German attacks. This meant weakening Germany and reducing its military strength. The French wanted revenge on Germany for the destruction the war had caused.
- Lloyd George wanted to protect British interests but was aware that treating Germany too harshly would store up trouble for the future. However, before the peace conference he had promised the British people that he would 'squeeze the German lemon until the pips squeak'.
- The 'Big Three' often disagreed. All were forced to compromise on their demands. The final treaties satisfied nobody.
- They agreed to set up a new international organisation – the League of Nations – which would work for peace.

Summary Box 1

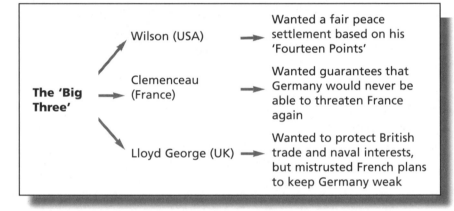

The Treaty of Versailles (1919)

- This was the name of the treaty that the Allies signed with Germany.
- Germany had to accept responsibility for the war – this was the 'War Guilt' clause.
- Germany would have to pay reparations for the damage caused by the war. In 1921 the Reparations Committee decided that Germany would have to pay £6600 million.
- Germany lost territory to France, Belgium, Denmark, and Lithuania. German land (the 'Polish Corridor') was taken to give Poland an outlet to the sea. Danzig and the Saar were put under control of the League of Nations, and the Rhineland was demilitarised. Union with Austria (Anschluss) was forbidden. All Germany's colonies passed into the hands of the League of Nations, who allocated them to other nations as mandates.
- Germany's armed forces were limited. The army could have no more than 100,000 men, with no tanks. The navy could have no battleships or submarines. Germany could have no air force.

Summary Box 2

According to the terms of the Treaty of Versailles, Germany had to:

- Accept responsibility for the war (War Guilt)
- Pay reparations
- Lose territory in Europe
- Lose all its colonies
- Limit its army to 100,000 men
- Limit the size of its navy
- Have no air force

The impact of the Treaty of Versailles on Germany to 1923

- The Germans did not expect a harsh treaty. They had already overthrown the Kaiser's government (which was responsible for the war) and had set up a new democratic republic. They expected a peace based on Wilson's 'Fourteen Points'.
- The Germans were dismayed by the terms of the Treaty of Versailles, which they condemned as harsh and unreasonable. They were not allowed to negotiate with the Allies. They called the treaty a 'diktat' – a dictated peace.
- Many Germans did not really accept that they had lost the war. They called the politicians who had made peace 'the November Criminals'. From the start, the Weimar Republic took the blame for agreeing to the treaty.
- Extremists tried to overthrow the Weimar Republic. The communist Spartacus League staged an unsuccessful revolution in 1919. In 1920 the extreme nationalist Freikorps, under Kapp, staged a putsch which failed only when socialist workers organised a general strike in favour of the government.
- When Germany delayed reparations payments, French and Belgian forces occupied Germany's most important industrial area, the Ruhr, in 1923. The German government ordered workers in the area to go on strike, and printed more money to pay them. This caused the German mark to lose its value (inflation).
- The Ruhr crisis caused the 'Great Inflation' of 1923 which left Germany bankrupt. But by the end of the year a new government under Stresemann brought the crisis to an end by accepting that reparations would have to be paid. In the next few years, with the help of US loans agreed in the Dawes Plan (1924), Weimar Germany recovered.

The other peace treaties

- The Treaty of St Germain (1919) was signed with Austria. It set out the terms for the break-up of the Austro-Hungarian Empire. Austria and Hungary became separate states, Czechoslovakia became independent, and land was lost to Romania and to the new states, Poland and Yugoslavia.

- The Treaty of Neuilly (1919) was signed with Bulgaria, which lost land to Yugoslavia and Greece.
- The Treaty of Trianon (1920) was signed with Hungary. This confirmed the land losses set out in the Treaty of St Germain.
- Austria, Bulgaria and Hungary all had to agree to pay reparations and to limit their armed forces.
- The Treaty of Sèvres (1920) was agreed with Turkey. This split up the Ottoman Empire. Arabia became independent and Turkey's other territories in the Middle East became League of Nations' mandates. However, the treaty was never ratified, because the Turks refused to accept proposed land losses to Greece, and it was amended by the Treaty of Lausanne (1923).

Summary Box 3

The other peace treaties

St Germain, signed with Austria (1919): broke up the Austro-Hungarian Empire and set up new states in Central Europe

Neuilly, signed with Bulgaria (1919): Bulgaria lost land to Greece and Yugoslavia

Trianon, signed with Hungary (1920): confirmed Hungary's land losses to Yugoslavia, Romania, Czechoslovakia and Poland agreed at St Germain

Sèvres, signed with Turkey (1920): Turkey lost land to Greece and its lands in the Middle East were handed over to the League as mandates. Losses to Greece were revoked in the Treaty of Lausanne (1923)

The impact of the peace treaties on the other defeated nations

- The break-up of the Austro-Hungarian Empire did not satisfy everyone. It was impossible to give self-determination to all the racial minorities of Central Europe. The new nations all contained resentful minorities who would cause trouble in future.
- The new states of Central Europe were small and weak. For a short time in 1919 Hungary was taken over by a communist government. The collapse of the Austrian and Hungarian economies in 1922–3 meant no reparations could be paid.
- The Turks resented the Treaty of Sèvres so much that they overthrew the Sultan, who was replaced by Mustapha Kemal. It was Kemal's government that negotiated the Treaty of Lausanne (see above) by which Turkey recovered the land lost to Greece.

Why did the victors not get everything they wanted?

- The 'Big Three' all wanted different things from the Treaty of Versailles, so they all had to compromise.

- During the war promises had been made to certain countries. For example, Italy had been promised territory to persuade it to join the war in 1915, and Japan's claims on China had been supported by the British. The victors had to keep some of these promises, even where they broke the principle of self-determination.

- When the Russian and Austrian Empires collapsed, national groups wanting independence, like the Czechs, did not wait for the peacemakers to tell them what to do. They set up their own governments, so that when the peace conference finally met, the map of Europe had already, to a great extent, been redrawn.

- When the Allies agreed an armistice (end of fighting) with Germany in November 1918, they insisted on very strict conditions so that fighting could not start again. Many of the terms of the Versailles Treaty, such as reparations, were actually agreed in the armistice, so the peacemakers were often dealing with issues which had already been agreed in principle.

- The 'Big Three' were under pressure from public opinion. None of them was free to act as he wished. This was especially true of Wilson, whose position was weakened by lack of support in the USA, and Lloyd George, who soon came to doubt the wisdom of punishing Germany, but had promised the British people that he would make Germany pay.

Were the treaties fair?

- The Germans did not think so. From the start they made every effort to convince the world that the terms were harsh and unfair.

- Many other people agreed with the Germans. In 1919, the British economist Keynes published a book criticising the idea of reparations. Many historians since have argued that the terms of the Versailles Treaty made future war more likely.

- However, many historians now think the peacemakers did a reasonable job in the circumstances. They point out that:
  - The problems facing the peacemakers were enormously complex, and given the demand for revenge against Germany, the terms of the treaties could have been harsher;
  - The Germans forced a much harsher peace on Russia (the Treaty of Brest-Litovsk) in March 1918;
  - In the Armistice, the Germans agreed to reductions in their armed forces, losses of territory and the principle of reparations. Why then did they seem surprised when these were included in the peace treaty?
  - The peacemakers set up the League of Nations. It was assumed the League would deal with any issues the treaties left unresolved.

What do I Know?

1. Who was the French representative in the 'Big Three'?
2. Who devised the 'Fourteen Points'?
3. What did the peacemakers mean by 'self-determination'?
4. Name the area given to Poland by the Versailles Treaty as an outlet to the sea.
5. What did the Versailles Treaty say about the Rhineland?
6. Which area did France regain from Germany in the Versailles Treaty?
7. What amount was demanded from Germany as reparations?
8. What limit was placed on the German army in the Versailles Treaty?
9. Which treaty was signed with Austria?
10. Which new state was created by giving land from the Austro-Hungarian Empire to Serbia?
11. Who took power in Turkey when the Sultan accepted the Treaty of Sèvres?
12. Which new state in Central Europe was temporarily taken over by communists during 1919?
13. Why did the Germans call the Treaty of Versailles a 'diktat'?
14. Which area did the French and Belgians occupy in 1923 when the Germans failed to make reparations payments?
15. What was the Dawes Plan (1924)?

My score …

Using the Sources

For this topic the only source-based question you might have to answer would be in Section A of Paper 1. Here is an example (remember that in the real examination these questions would have a part (b) too, but it is not source-based).

Source A

DER TAG!

▶ A cartoon about the Treaty of Versailles published in a British newspaper, May 1919.

(a) Study Source A. Explain the message of this cartoon. Support your answer by referring to details of the cartoon and your knowledge. **(6 marks)**

Explaining the message of a cartoon never means simply stating what the cartoon shows. You have to interpret the cartoon – understand what it's about. Here you need to know who the 'Big Four' are, and what they are doing. Who is the person held in the hand, and why does he have to swallow the peace terms? Given what you have already learnt about the Treaty of Versailles it should be fairly obvious to you what is going on, but there's still a knack to earning the highest possible mark in your answer. Not only do you have to explain what is happening, you must *use* details of the cartoon to back up your explanation. Finally, you should also make sure that your explanation demonstrates your knowledge of the topic. This does not mean writing everything you know about Versailles, but it does mean adding details which are not in the cartoon in order to explain its message. For example, you could point out that one of the reasons the man (Germany) is struggling so much is because he will have to pay reparations (that's why the pills are 'worth millions a box'). Nowhere does the cartoon state the word reparations, so by using it in your explanation you have demonstrated additional knowledge.

Have a go at answering the question for yourself.

Exam Type Question

Section B of Paper 1 consists of structured questions on the Core Content. Here is an example on the peace treaties.

> (a) What restrictions did the Treaty of Versailles place on Germany's armed forces? **(4 marks)**
>
> (b) Explain why France wanted a harsh peace to be imposed on Germany. **(6 marks)**
>
> (c) How far do you agree that the Treaty of Versailles was unfair on Germany? Explain your answer. **(10 marks)**

Have a go yourself at parts (a) and (b), but here are a couple of students' answers to part (c).

Answer 1

I think the treaty was very unfair on Germany. The Germans had got rid of the Kaiser and their new government was trying to make a fresh start – they weren't to blame for starting the war. Demanding so much reparations was a stupid mistake. The British economist Keynes said it would just make Germany broke so that it wouldn't be able to trade with anyone, and that would make everyone poorer. But of course the French wanted to make sure that

Germany couldn't recover, that was the whole point. The British and the Americans didn't want the treaty to be so tough but Clemenceau got his way and Germany was punished in all kinds of ways. It was bound to make Germany resentful and it did a lot to cause the Second World War because the Germans never really accepted it.

Answer 2

Lots of people have agreed that the treaty was unfair on Germany. You can see why they thought this because the Germans were forced to accept it. The treaty was not negotiated, but was imposed on Germany. This was unusual with peace treaties and, given that many Germans didn't really believe that their armies had been completely defeated, was bound to cause resentment in Germany. The terms also look harsh. The military restrictions, for example, meant that Germany was reduced to the status of a small, insignificant nation. Lloyd George knew that trying to take revenge on Germany was bound to store up trouble in the future but the French were determined to keep Germany down. However, in some ways the Germans had themselves to blame. In the Treaty of Brest-Litovsk, the Germans took so much land from Russia that a quarter of Russia's population was lost. So when they had the chance to impose terms on an enemy, they showed no mercy. And in order to get peace, they had already agreed to harsh terms in the armistice agreement, so the final treaty can't have been that much of a surprise to them. Overall, most historians today don't regard the treaty as particularly unfair. They think that the peacemakers did a reasonable job in difficult circumstances, and that the Germans were not treated too harshly.

Examiner's Comments: Answer 1

6 out of 10

This answer identifies and explains several reasons why the treaty could be seen as unfair. The knowledge demonstrated is accurate, but the answer is limited because it looks at only one side of the question. It assumes the treaty was unfair and does not consider any arguments to the contrary. Without a balanced argument, an answer to part (c) questions can never achieve the highest marks.

Answer 2

10 out of 10

You can see straight away that this answer looks at both sides of the question. There are explanations here both of why the treaty could be seen as unfair and why it was fair. This alone will score a high mark, but the answer goes a step further by adding a balanced conclusion on 'how far?' the treaty was unfair.

1.2 To what extent was the League of Nations a success?

Topic Summary

The League of Nations was seriously weakened by the USA's decision not to join. Despite this, during the 1920s it did much good work, both in dealing with international disputes and, through its commissions and agencies, in coping with a range of social and economic problems. However, the Great Depression, which started in 1929, led to a much more dangerous international situation. Even in the 1920s the League had shown weakness in dealing with aggressors and its failure to cope with the crises over Manchuria (1931–3) and Abyssinia (1935–6) led directly to its downfall.

What do I Need to Know?

You will need to understand the reasons for the weaknesses of the League. You will need to be able to judge how much success the League had during the 1920s, and explain why the international situation worsened during the 1930s. Most importantly, you will need to understand why the League failed so completely to deal with the aggression of Japan and Italy in Manchuria and Abyssinia.

Key Topics

The structure and organisation of the League

- The League was created by the peace treaties after the First World War. The Covenant of the League was included in all the peace treaties.
- The aims of the League were contained in its Covenant.
- The League was based in Geneva, Switzerland. It started work in January 1920.
- The Assembly was the League's parliament. All nations sent representatives to it.
- The Council was a smaller committee that made most major decisions. Britain, France, Japan and Italy were permanent members of the Council.
- The Secretariat was the civil service of the League.
- Special Commissions were set up to deal with a range of issues, such as disarmament, drugs, refugees, health, women's rights and the mandates.
- The Permanent Court of Justice in The Hague ruled on international legal problems.
- At first 42 nations were members, but this number increased as time went on.

What weaknesses were there in the structure and organisation of the League?

- Not all nations were members of the League. The USA never joined. The defeated nations, like Germany, were not members at first. Other nations left when they got into disputes with the League.
- The League had no armed forces of its own. It relied on *collective security* – that is, the willingness of its members to work together to deal with aggression. Too often, this meant nations looked to the League to take action when they weren't willing to act themselves.
- The League was dominated by Britain and France, but they never really agreed on how powerful it should be.
- The League was too slow to take action. All decisions, in the Assembly and the Council, had to be taken unanimously.
- The League was too idealistic. It was unrealistic to expect nations to obey the League without giving it the power to enforce its will.

Summary Box 1

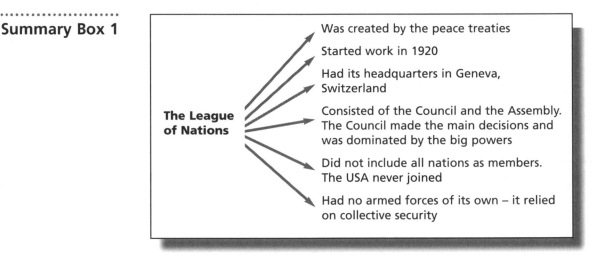

The League of Nations

- Was created by the peace treaties
- Started work in 1920
- Had its headquarters in Geneva, Switzerland
- Consisted of the Council and the Assembly. The Council made the main decisions and was dominated by the big powers
- Did not include all nations as members. The USA never joined
- Had no armed forces of its own – it relied on collective security

How far was the League successful in the 1920s?

The League had a mixed record in dealing with international disputes during the 1920s. It was reasonably successful in disputes between small nations, but the Corfu dispute was an early example of its weakness when stronger nations were involved.

Main successes

- It resolved the Aaland Islands dispute between Sweden and Finland (1921).
- It arranged international help to prevent the collapse of the Austrian and Hungarian economies (1922–3).
- It arranged a plebiscite over Upper Silesia (1921), and decided to partition the area between Germany and Poland.
- It settled the Greek–Bulgarian frontier dispute (1925).

Main failures

- It could do nothing about the Polish occupation of Vilna, an area of Lithuania seized by the Poles in 1920.
- It did nothing to prevent Italian aggression against Greece in a dispute over Corfu, a Greek island (1923). Instead the Great Powers pressurised the Greeks to pay Italy compensation.

The Great Powers continued to make agreements without involving the League, even when these involved armament issues, such as the Washington Naval agreement of 1922, or related directly to the Paris peace treaties, such as the Locarno agreements of 1925.

During the 1920s the Commissions of the League carried out much useful humanitarian work in helping refugees, fighting against slavery, and organising health and education campaigns. However, the Disarmament Commission found it impossible to make progress. The Disarmament Conference of 1932–3 collapsed and led directly to Germany leaving the League.

Summary Box 2

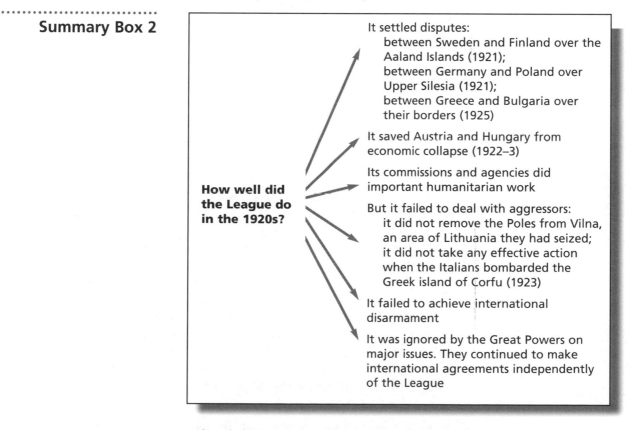

How well did the League do in the 1920s?

It settled disputes:
between Sweden and Finland over the Aaland Islands (1921);
between Germany and Poland over Upper Silesia (1921);
between Greece and Bulgaria over their borders (1925)

It saved Austria and Hungary from economic collapse (1922–3)

Its commissions and agencies did important humanitarian work

But it failed to deal with aggressors:
it did not remove the Poles from Vilna, an area of Lithuania they had seized;
it did not take any effective action when the Italians bombarded the Greek island of Corfu (1923)

It failed to achieve international disarmament

It was ignored by the Great Powers on major issues. They continued to make international agreements independently of the League

Why did the Depression make the work of the League more difficult?

- The world economic crisis caused by the Great Depression had political consequences.
- Millions of people around the world lost their jobs. In their desperation, they turned to extreme political parties that promised solutions to the economic crisis.

- These extremist parties, like the Nazis in Germany, were often *nationalist* in nature. They did not believe in democracy and international co-operation. Rather, they hated other countries and cared only for themselves. They ignored the authority of the League.
- Another aspect of extreme nationalism was *militarism*. These parties built up their armed forces, and used aggression against other nations to achieve their ends. The world thus began the descent into violence which led to the Second World War.

Why did the League fail in Manchuria and Abyssinia?

Failure over Manchuria (1931–3)

- In September 1931 the Mukden Incident occurred. The Japanese army used the excuse of an explosion on the South Manchurian railway outside Mukden to begin the occupation of the whole of Manchuria.
- China appealed for the League's help. It seemed an obvious case of aggression.
- The League instructed Japan to withdraw, but was ignored. The Japanese completed the occupation of Manchuria, which they renamed Manchukuo. They installed Pu Yi, the last Chinese Emperor, as a puppet ruler.
- The League set up the Lytton Commission. Its report in 1932 condemned Japan's actions. When the League accepted the report, Japan left the League. The League took no further action.

Why did the League fail to prevent Japanese aggression?

- There was little the League could actually do. It had no way to force Japan to withdraw. Japan was a powerful nation and was determined to ignore the League.
- For most League members, events in East Asia seemed very distant. The League was very eurocentric in its attitudes. It did not look on an Asian crisis as being as vital as one in Europe.
- Everyone accepted that Japan had legitimate economic interests in Manchuria. It was seen as a Japanese sphere of interest.
- China was very weak at the time. Some League members welcomed the fact that Japan was imposing 'order' on Manchuria.

Failure over Abyssinia (1935–6)

- In October 1935, Italy started an invasion of Abyssinia. It had been clear for at least a year – since the clash between the two countries in December 1934 at the oasis of Wal Wal – that Italy was planning an invasion.
- The Abyssinian forces stood little chance of resisting the modern Italian army and air force, which used tanks, bombers and poison gas against opponents often armed only with spears.
- The League condemned Italy, and imposed sanctions. Crucially these did not include restrictions on oil and other war materials.

- Behind the scenes Britain and France searched desperately for a solution to the crisis. The Hoare–Laval Plan to partition Abyssinia was leaked to the press, and both men had to resign, but it showed that the British and French were not prepared to back tough action.
- Abyssinia was abandoned and by May 1936 Italian troops had completed the conquest.
- The Abyssinian emperor, Haile Selassie, escaped and travelled to Geneva where, in June 1936, he addressed the Assembly of the League, protesting against its failure to protect his country.
- The League's failure over Abyssinia was a disaster. Nobody took it seriously from then on.

Why did the League fail to deal with Italian aggression?

- Britain and France were desperate to keep Italy's friendship. They were worried that Mussolini would ally Italy with Hitler's Germany.
- Britain and France had colonies in Africa. To many people it did not seem so unreasonable that Italy should be allowed to colonise Abyssinia.
- France had made secret agreements with Mussolini giving him economic concessions in North Africa. Mussolini may have thought France would not object to him taking over Abyssinia.
- Britain and France were not willing to risk war with Mussolini. Nobody else in the League was strong enough to resist him.

Summary Box 3

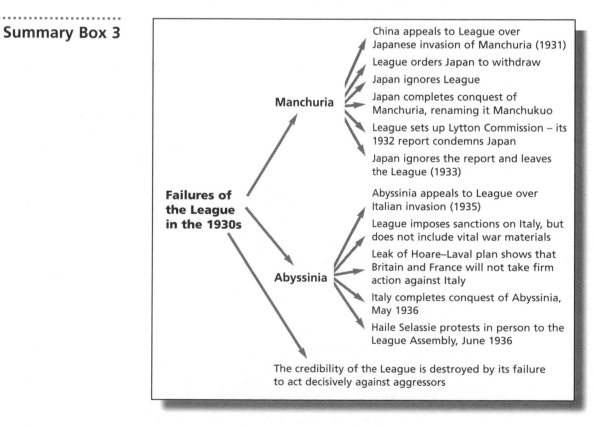

Failures of the League in the 1930s

Manchuria
- China appeals to League over Japanese invasion of Manchuria (1931)
- League orders Japan to withdraw
- Japan ignores League
- Japan completes conquest of Manchuria, renaming it Manchukuo
- League sets up Lytton Commission – its 1932 report condemns Japan
- Japan ignores the report and leaves the League (1933)

Abyssinia
- Abyssinia appeals to League over Italian invasion (1935)
- League imposes sanctions on Italy, but does not include vital war materials
- Leak of Hoare–Laval plan shows that Britain and France will not take firm action against Italy
- Italy completes conquest of Abyssinia, May 1936
- Haile Selassie protests in person to the League Assembly, June 1936

The credibility of the League is destroyed by its failure to act decisively against aggressors

**What do
I Know?**

1 In which year did the League start its work?
2 Name the document which set out the aims of the League.
3 Where did the Permanent Court of Justice meet?
4 Name any **three** of the Special Commissions of the League.
5 How many members did the League have when it started?
6 Name a Great Power that was not a member of the League when it started.
7 Which Great Power left the League in 1933 over the collapse of the Disarmament Conference?
8 Which two nations were in dispute over the Aaland Islands?
9 What was the result of the plebiscite over Upper Silesia held in March 1921?
10 Name the Italian dictator who was responsible for the bombardment and occupation of Corfu (1923).
11 Who did the Japanese choose as the puppet ruler of Manchuria after their conquest?
12 What name was given to Manchuria by the Japanese after their invasion?
13 Name the Commission of Inquiry set up by the League to report on the invasion of Manchuria.
14 At which oasis did a clash occur between Italian and Abyssinian troops in December 1934?
15 Name the Emperor of Abyssinia who fled his country because of the Italian invasion.

My score ...

What was the importance of:

• the Council of the League

• collective security

• the Mukden Incident

• the Hoare–Laval Plan?

**Using the
Sources**

For this topic the only source-based question you might have to answer would be in Section A of Paper 1. Source A on page 21 is an example (remember that in the real examination these questions would have a part (b) too, but it is not source-based).

(a) Study Source A. Explain the message of this cartoon. Support your answer by referring to details of the cartoon and your knowledge.   **(6 marks)**

There are six marks available on these questions. To earn these marks you are going to have to do all three things required by the question: that is *explain* what the cartoon is saying (in other words, *interpret* the cartoon), *use* details of the cartoon to back up your interpretation, and *use* your background knowledge to make sense of the details of the cartoon. So, to answer the first aspect of the question, I could say, 'The message of the cartoon is that the League was useless in dealing with the Manchurian crisis.' Then I could back this up by saying, 'I can tell this from the cartoon because you can see that Japan is making a face at the League – all the lawyers can do

Source A

▲ **A British cartoon about the response of the League of Nations to the Japanese invasion of Manchuria.**

is shiver and read the Lytton Report.' So far I haven't used any of my own knowledge, so finally I would add, 'The Lytton Commission of Inquiry looked into the Japanese invasion and produced a report condemning Japan, but the Japanese just ignored it and left the League. This shows the cartoon was right in saying the League was useless.'

Have a go at answering the question for yourself, but use your own interpretation and different supporting details! There's plenty of other material in the cartoon to use.

Exam Type Question

Section B of Paper 1 consists of structured questions on the Core Content. Here is an example on the League of Nations.

> **(a)** What were the main weaknesses in the structure and organisation of the League of Nations? **(4 marks)**
>
> **(b)** Explain why the League failed to take decisive action against Japan over the invasion of Manchuria. **(6 marks)**
>
> **(c)** How far do you agree that the League failed miserably to achieve its aims? Explain your answer. **(10 marks)**

Have a go yourself at parts (b) and (c), but here are a couple of students' answers to part (a).

Answer 1

The main weaknesses of the League were that it had no army, all decisions had to be unanimous, and it was dominated by Britain and France.

Answer 2

The League had several important weaknesses. One of the most important was that it did not include all nations, so that a Great Power like the USA never was a member, and other countries like Germany weren't members all the time. Another weakness was that the League was slow to take action. All decisions, both in the Council and the Assembly, had to be unanimous, which was difficult to achieve as nations were bound to disagree.

Examiner's Comments: Answer 1

3 out of 4

This answer identifies three clear weaknesses relating to the structure and organisation of the League. In part (a) questions, which are intended to test your powers of recall, one mark will be given for each relevant point made. So this answer would score three out of four marks – the additional mark could have been gained by adding one more point (for example, that not all nations were members).

Answer 2

4 out of 4

You can see that this is a different kind of answer from the first one. There are only two weaknesses given, but additional detail is provided for both. The marking scheme rewards this kind of answer too. You would score two marks for the two weaknesses, but answers can also be awarded one extra mark for the supporting detail applied to each point.

1.3 Why had international peace collapsed by 1939?

Topic Summary

The Treaty of Versailles left the Germans resentful and determined to reverse its terms. One of Hitler's main aims in foreign policy was to destroy the treaty and within only a couple of years of taking power in 1933 he had done so. His aggressive actions threatened the peace of Europe. At first Britain and France followed a policy of appeasement to try to satisfy Germany's demands, but successive crises in 1938-9 over Austria, Czechoslovakia and Poland led rapidly to the outbreak of war in September 1939.

What do I Need to Know?

You will need to understand how and why Hitler was able to destroy the Versailles Treaty so easily. You should be able to explain why Britain and France followed a policy of appeasement, and to appreciate the advantages and disadvantages of this policy. You will need to know the steps towards war which occurred in Europe from 1933 onwards, and be able to explain the significance of key events like the remilitarisation of the Rhineland, the Munich Conference and the Nazi–Soviet Pact.

Key Topics

What were the long-term consequences of the peace treaties of 1919–23?

- The peace treaties left many nations dissatisfied with what they had lost or gained.
- These nations wanted to revise the peace settlement of 1919-23.
- The most important of these dissatisfied nations was Germany. Almost all Germans wanted to reject the Treaty of Versailles.
- The impact of the Great Depression brought militarist extremists to power in many countries.
- In Germany, Hitler's rise to power was assisted by his promise to destroy the Versailles Treaty.
- Hitler's aggressive demands, such as his desire for 'lebensraum' (living space) for the German people, seemed to threaten war in Europe.
- Britain and France responded to these threats with a policy of appeasement – trying to satisfy Germany's demands in order to preserve peace.

How did Hitler destroy the Treaty of Versailles?

- In October 1933 Germany left the Disarmament Conference and quit the League of Nations.

- In January 1935, the people of the Saar voted overwhelmingly to rejoin Germany.
- In March 1935 Hitler announced that Germany had an air force, and was introducing conscription – both forbidden by the Versailles Treaty. In response, Britain, France and Italy formed the 'Stresa Front', to try to preserve existing treaties.
- In June 1935 the Anglo-German Naval Treaty was signed. This allowed Germany to rebuild its navy to 35 per cent of the strength of the British navy, and showed that Britain no longer upheld the military terms of the Versailles Treaty.
- In March 1936 Germany remilitarised the Rhineland. Britain and France made no effort to stop Germany 'marching into its own backyard'.
- The Rome–Berlin Axis (1936) with Italy, and the Anti-Comintern Pacts (1936, 1937) with Japan and Italy, indicated that Germany was ready to develop friendships with other extremist militaristic countries. Germany's friendship with Italy became a formal military alliance, with the Pact of Steel signed in 1939.

Summary Box 1

Hitler destroys the Versailles Treaty

1933: Germany leaves the Disarmament Conference and quits the League

1935: Saar plebiscite regains German territory

1935: Hitler announces German re-armament

1935: Anglo-German Naval Treaty signed

1936: remilitarisation of the Rhineland

1936: Rome–Berlin Axis formed

How far was Hitler's foreign policy to blame for the outbreak of war in 1939?

Austria

- During an attempted coup by the Nazis in 1934, the Austrian Chancellor, Dolfuss, was murdered. The coup failed only because Mussolini would not support it.
- In January 1938 Austrian police discovered another Nazi plot to take over the government.
- To try and preserve Austria's independence, Schuschnigg, the Chancellor, agreed to let Nazis join his government. He hoped this would appease Hitler.
- However, Schuschnigg also announced a plebiscite allowing the Austrians to vote on whether they wanted to remain independent or not.
- Hitler was worried that the plebiscite would prevent him taking over Austria, so on 12 March 1938 he invaded.
- On 10 April 1938, the Austrians voted by over 99 per cent to approve the Anschluss (the union of Austria with Germany).

Czechoslovakia

- The border area between Germany and Czechoslovakia – the Sudetenland – contained over 3 million Germans. Hitler demanded that the Sudetenland be given to Germany.
- Without the Sudetenland, Czechoslovakia would be defenceless against German attack.
- Chamberlain, the British Prime Minister, wanted to find a peaceful solution to the Sudetenland problem. Neither Britain nor France was prepared to fight Germany over Czechoslovakia.
- On 15 September 1938 Chamberlain met Hitler at Berchtesgaden. Chamberlain agreed Hitler could have the Sudetenland as long as the transfer was done peacefully.
- A week later, the two men met again, this time at Bad Godesberg. This time Hitler demanded handover of the Sudetenland by 1 October 1938, or there would be war.
- On 29 September 1938, Chamberlain and Hitler met with Mussolini and Daladier (the French Prime Minister) in Munich. The British and French gave Hitler what he had demanded at Bad Godesberg. The Czechs were forced to accept the agreement.
- The following day, Hitler and Chamberlain signed an Anglo-German Declaration promising that their countries would never go to war, and would settle any disputes between them peacefully. When Chamberlain returned to Britain he said, 'I believe it is peace for our time.'
- During October–November, Hungary and Poland also seized parts of Czech territory.
- In March 1939, Hitler took over the rest of Czechoslovakia. His armies occupied Bohemia and Moravia, whilst Slovakia became a German 'puppet state'.
- It was clear that appeasement had failed. Britain promised Poland, Hitler's next target, that Britain would guarantee its independence.

Poland

- In the Treaty of Versailles, Germany had lost the 'Polish corridor' and Danzig. Hitler wanted these back.
- Poland, made bolder by Britain's guarantee, refused to negotiate with Hitler.
- During 1939, the British, French and Soviets negotiated over how to defend Poland. The negotiations failed because of mutual mistrust and the Poles' unwillingness to let Soviet troops into their territory.
- The announcement of the Nazi–Soviet Pact, signed by the Foreign Ministers of the two countries, Ribbentrop and Molotov, on 23 August 1939 meant that Poland was doomed. Secretly, Germany and the USSR had agreed to split Poland between them.
- Hitler now knew he could invade Poland without the interference of the Great Powers. Britain and France were too far away to intervene.

- Hitler's invasion of Poland on 1 September 1939 forced Britain and France to declare war two days later. Britain had guaranteed Poland's independence, but this did not save Poland which, within three weeks, had ceased to exist.

Summary Box 2

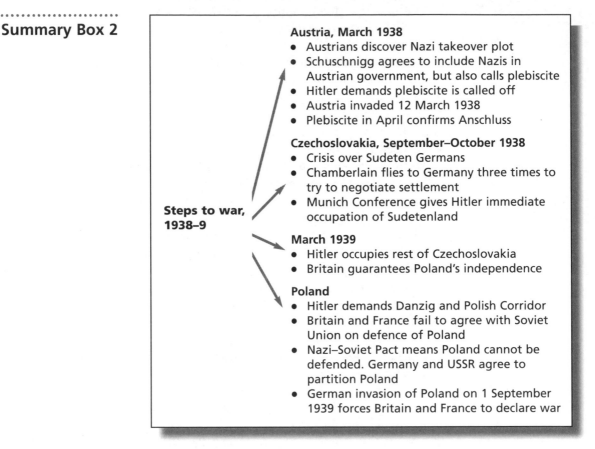

Steps to war, 1938–9

Austria, March 1938
- Austrians discover Nazi takeover plot
- Schuschnigg agrees to include Nazis in Austrian government, but also calls plebiscite
- Hitler demands plebiscite is called off
- Austria invaded 12 March 1938
- Plebiscite in April confirms Anschluss

Czechoslovakia, September–October 1938
- Crisis over Sudeten Germans
- Chamberlain flies to Germany three times to try to negotiate settlement
- Munich Conference gives Hitler immediate occupation of Sudetenland

March 1939
- Hitler occupies rest of Czechoslovakia
- Britain guarantees Poland's independence

Poland
- Hitler demands Danzig and Polish Corridor
- Britain and France fail to agree with Soviet Union on defence of Poland
- Nazi–Soviet Pact means Poland cannot be defended. Germany and USSR agree to partition Poland
- German invasion of Poland on 1 September 1939 forces Britain and France to declare war

Was Britain's policy of appeasement justified?

Appeasement failed to avoid war. However, historians still argue over whether or not the policy was justified.

Arguments in favour of appeasement

- The Treaty of Versailles was too harsh on Germany, and it was simply common sense to try to settle Germany's grievances by negotiation.
- It was correct to try to avoid war. Memories of the First World War were very fresh, and it was natural for British politicians to be horrified by the thought of more bloodshed.
- It is easy with hindsight to see Hitler as the main threat. At the time it was not so simple. Stalin's communist tyranny in the Soviet Union seemed equally dangerous. Many British politicians were tempted to see a strong Germany as a useful protection against the USSR.
- Britain was not ready to fight Germany. Rearmament really got under way only in 1936. Appeasement gave Britain time to re-arm.

Arguments against appeasement

- Appeasement was wrong. It was another word for cowardice and giving in to the demands of a bully.
- The appeasers assumed that, if they made concessions to Hitler, it would reduce the chances of war. In fact it did the opposite. By showing weakness, they just encouraged Hitler to demand more.
- The appeasers assumed Hitler was just another rational politician with whom they could negotiate on equal terms. They completely misjudged his ruthlessness and his willingness both to break agreements and to use force to gain his ends.
- The appeasers missed vital opportunities to stop Hitler. In particular, had they resisted the remilitarisation of the Rhineland, Hitler would probably have withdrawn his forces, which were not ready for war.
- In 1938, by abandoning Czechoslovakia, Britain lost a potentially important ally against Hitler.

Summary Box 3

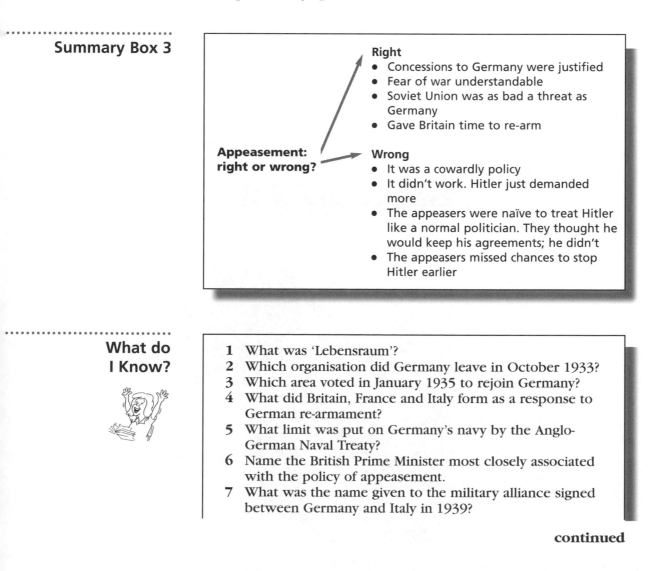

Appeasement: right or wrong?

Right
- Concessions to Germany were justified
- Fear of war understandable
- Soviet Union was as bad a threat as Germany
- Gave Britain time to re-arm

Wrong
- It was a cowardly policy
- It didn't work. Hitler just demanded more
- The appeasers were naïve to treat Hitler like a normal politician. They thought he would keep his agreements; he didn't
- The appeasers missed chances to stop Hitler earlier

What do I Know?

1 What was 'Lebensraum'?
2 Which organisation did Germany leave in October 1933?
3 Which area voted in January 1935 to rejoin Germany?
4 What did Britain, France and Italy form as a response to German re-armament?
5 What limit was put on Germany's navy by the Anglo-German Naval Treaty?
6 Name the British Prime Minister most closely associated with the policy of appeasement.
7 What was the name given to the military alliance signed between Germany and Italy in 1939?

continued

8 What was the 'Anschluss'?

9 Name the Austrian chancellor murdered by Nazis in 1934.

10 Which Austrian chancellor offered the Austrian people a plebiscite in 1938 on maintaining their independence?

11 What was the Sudetenland?

12 Name the two places in Germany where Chamberlain met Hitler in September 1938 prior to the Munich Conference.

13 Which two countries other than Germany seized land from Czechoslovakia in October–November 1938?

14 Which country's independence did Britain guarantee in March 1939?

15 Which two men signed the Nazi–Soviet Pact on behalf of Germany and the USSR?

My score …

What was the importance of:

- the remilitarisation of the Rhineland
- the Rome-Berlin Axis
- the Munich Agreement
- the Nazi–Soviet Pact?

Using the Sources

For this topic the only source-based question you might have to answer would be in Section A of Paper 1. Here is an example (remember that in the real examination these questions would have a part (b) too, but it is not source-based).

Source A

▼ A Soviet cartoon of 1939. It shows Chamberlain and Daladier dressed as policemen. The signpost says Western Europe to the left and the Soviet Union to the right.

(a) Study Source A on page 28. Explain the message of this cartoon. Support your answer by referring to details of the cartoon and your knowledge. **(6 marks)**

First, identify the point that the Soviet cartoonist is making. The cartoon illustrates Soviet fears about how Britain and France wanted to use German strength to crush the USSR. Put this message into your own words, and then show how features of the cartoon – for example, how Chamberlain and Daladier are pointing down the road to the Soviet Union – can be used to support the message. Finally (and without this you cannot get full marks), explain features of the cartoon using your own knowledge. This must be knowledge which the cartoon itself does not provide. Here, for example, you could mention how talks between Britain, France and the Soviet Union during 1939 failed to agree on how to protect Poland because of the Soviet belief that they would have to do all the fighting against Germany in the event of an invasion.

Have a go at answering question (a) for yourself, but put the interpretation into your own words and use different supporting details. There are several points which you could mention.

Exam Type Question

Section B of Paper 1 consists of structured questions on the Core Content. Here is an example on the causes of the Second World War in Europe.

> (a) What was appeasement? **(4 marks)**
>
> (b) Explain why Britain and France agreed at the Munich Conference to give Germany the Sudetenland. **(6 marks)**
>
> (c) How far do you agree that the Nazi–Soviet Pact was the most important cause of war in September 1939? Explain your answer. **(10 marks)**

Have a go yourself at parts (a) and (c), but here are a couple of students' answers to part (b).

Answer 1

Britain and France agreed to give Germany the Sudetenland because it was mainly inhabited by German people. This persuaded Chamberlain that the German demand for the area had some justice to it, so he persuaded the Czechs to give the area up. There were other reasons too, like they were afraid of war.

Answer 2

> The Munich agreement was an example of appeasement. By giving Hitler the Sudetenland Britain and France hoped they would satisfy Hitler so that he would make no further demands and war would be avoided. Of course, they couldn't give in to any old demand just because he made it. It was important to make out that the demand had some sense to it and could be justified. With the Sudetenland this was true. Many Germans lived there, so Chamberlain could say he was giving them self-determination. There was a less noble reason too. Britain and France believed there was nothing they could do to save Czechoslovakia. They thought it was too far away to protect. They called it a 'far-away country of which we know little'.

Examiner's Comments: Answer 1

4 out of 6

In part (b) questions, marks are earned by *identifying* and *explaining* reasons. This answer identifies two reasons and explains one of them (identifying a reason means just giving the reason without saying why it mattered, or how it worked). The reason here that is only identified is that Britain and France were afraid of war. The explained reason is that the Sudetenland was inhabited by Germans and so Hitler's claim to the region could be justified. You can earn no more than three of the six marks for simply identifying two or more reasons – you have to explain the reasons to get higher marks.

Answer 2

6 out of 6

You should quickly realise that this is a better answer than the first example. It contains three clear reasons: Britain and France hoped appeasement would stop Hitler making more demands, many Germans lived in the Sudetenland, and they thought they could not defend Czechoslovakia from attack. Each of these reasons is well explained. It is possible to score full marks by giving just two explained reasons, as long as these are done well. This answer has made absolutely sure by giving three!

1.4 Who was to blame for the Cold War?

Topic Summary

As the Second World War came to an end, the alliance between the capitalist USA and the communist USSR began to fall apart. Now that they no longer had a common enemy in Germany, they could revert to their traditional hostility. At the Yalta and Potsdam peace conferences, disputes over the future of eastern Europe began to emerge. The USA suspected the USSR of trying to spread communism to as many countries as possible, while the USSR suspected that the West wanted to encourage German recovery in order to threaten Soviet security. To prevent any expansion of the 'Iron Curtain', the USA adopted a policy of 'containment'. In 1947 it announced the Truman Doctrine and the Marshall Plan. A 'Cold War' between East and West was now under way, and matters came to a head over the Berlin blockade of 1948-9. Although Stalin eventually backed down, the setting up of NATO in 1949 indicated that the West now regarded the USSR as the main threat to peace.

What do I Need to Know?

You will need to understand why the wartime alliance broke down, and what the traditional causes of hostility between the USA and the USSR were. You should know how and why the USSR came to dominate much of eastern Europe. You will need to be able to explain how the USA reacted to the setting up of the Iron Curtain, and to discuss the significance of developments such as the Truman Doctrine, Marshall Plan and Berlin blockade. The fundamental issue to consider is whether either side was more to blame than the other for the Cold War.

Key Topics

Why did the USA–USSR alliance begin to break down in 1945?

- With Germany defeated, the USA and the USSR no longer had a common enemy to fear.
- There was a history of hostility by the West towards the Soviet Union: the West had intervened in the Russian Civil War (1919–20) to try to stop the Bolshevik takeover; during the 1930s Stalin suspected that the West hoped to use Hitler to crush Soviet communism; during the Second World War Stalin felt the West deliberately delayed in launching a second front against Germany so that the USSR would have to do more than its fair share of the fighting against Germany.

- The different ideologies of the two countries – capitalism and communism – made it hard for them to trust each other.

COMMUNISM v CAPITALISM

Communism	Capitalism
• Communists believe in the ideas of Karl Marx (Marxists)	• Capitalists believe in capitalism (free markets)
• Industry and agriculture are owned by the state	• Industry and agriculture are in private hands
• Nobody makes profits and workers are paid by the state	• Businessmen make profits and pay their workers wages
• In a classless society all people are equal	• Class-based society, with rich and poor
• The state provides everything: schools, hospitals, housing, etc.	• Individuals have to provide for themselves
• No political freedoms, one-party state	• Political freedoms, many political parties

---

- **The Yalta Conference (1945)**, attended by Stalin, Roosevelt and Churchill, split Germany into four zones of occupation. It was also agreed that the USSR would permit free elections to set up new governments in the countries of eastern Europe that it had liberated. In practice, the West accepted that eastern Europe would be a Soviet sphere of influence. The main problem was Poland where Stalin wanted a pro-Soviet government, known as the 'Lublin Poles', to take over. He also wanted to keep Polish territory seized after the Nazi–Soviet Pact and to push the Polish frontier west. Roosevelt was reluctant to agree, but there was little the West could do in areas held by the Red Army. The Conference agreed to set up the United Nations Organisation.

- **The Potsdam Conference (1945)** was attended by the new US President, Harry Truman, by Stalin, and by the new British Prime Minister, Clement Attlee. Truman was much more suspicious of Stalin than Roosevelt had been. He demanded that the USSR allow free elections in eastern Europe, as promised at Yalta, but Stalin would not agree. Stalin also demanded that Germany should be crippled economically by severe reparations, and that the USSR should be allowed to take part in the occupation of Japan. Truman refused on both counts. But some things were agreed: the division of Germany into four zones was confirmed, Poland's new eastern border was fixed along the Oder–Neisse Line, and it was agreed that Germans living in Poland, Hungary and Czechoslovakia would be sent back to Germany.

- The worsening relations between the USSR and the USA came out into the open in 1946 when Winston Churchill made his famous 'Iron Curtain' speech in Fulton, Missouri. He accused the USSR of dividing Europe by an 'iron curtain' behind which all countries were dominated by the USSR and were denied freedom and democracy.

Summary Box 1

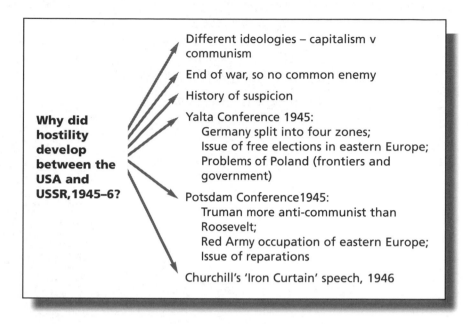

Why did hostility develop between the USA and USSR, 1945–6?

- Different ideologies – capitalism v communism
- End of war, so no common enemy
- History of suspicion
- Yalta Conference 1945:
  Germany split into four zones;
  Issue of free elections in eastern Europe;
  Problems of Poland (frontiers and government)
- Potsdam Conference 1945:
  Truman more anti-communist than Roosevelt;
  Red Army occupation of eastern Europe;
  Issue of reparations
- Churchill's 'Iron Curtain' speech, 1946

How had the USSR gained control of eastern Europe by 1948?

- The Soviet Union had been invaded from the West twice in 30 years. Stalin was determined to set up a 'buffer zone' to make sure this never happened again.
- The Red Army liberated eastern Europe from the Nazis. The Red Army remained in these countries to make sure that their new governments were communist-controlled.
  - The Baltic States (Estonia, Latvia, Lithuania) were annexed by the USSR.
  - Poland: the USSR annexed much of eastern Poland, and the Poles' western frontier was moved to the Oder–Neisse Line. Despite the USSR's promise to allow free elections, by 1947 Poland was totally in communist hands.
  - Romania: in 1945 the King was forced by the USSR to appoint a communist prime minister. This quickly led to a total communist takeover, and in 1947 the monarchy was abolished.
  - Bulgaria: in November 1945 the communists won a rigged election, and in 1946 abolished the monarchy.
  - Czechoslovakia: a coalition government took power after the war. Gradually, the communists undermined the government. In 1948 the Foreign Minister, Jan Masaryk, was murdered. Rigged elections followed. The communists won and banned all other parties.
  - East Germany: this was the Soviet zone of occupation as agreed at Yalta and Potsdam. In 1949, following the Berlin Blockade, it became the German Democratic Republic.
  - Hungary: in 1945 a free election led to the defeat of the communists. New rigged elections were held in 1947. The communists won and banned all opposition.

- Yugoslavia was not liberated by the Red Army. Instead its own communist resistance leader, Tito, set up a government and was elected President. Yugoslavia became a communist state, but would not accept Stalin's orders.

▼ **Soviet expansion 1945–80.**

How did the USA react to Soviet expansion?

- The USA interpreted the Soviet takeover of eastern Europe as the start of an attempt to spread communism around the world.
- The USA's immediate worry was that Greece and Turkey might be the next countries to fall to Stalin. When Britain said it could no longer afford to station troops in these countries, Truman decided to act.

- On 12 March 1947, Truman announced that the USA would give support to any free peoples struggling to avoid communist takeover. This was the Truman Doctrine.
- Truman also realised that governments in Europe – which were facing economic collapse and still struggling to cope with the after-effects of the war – were vulnerable to communist takeover.
- In June 1947, George Marshall, the US Secretary of State, announced a huge plan of economic aid to help build up Europe's economy. This was the Marshall Plan.
- Marshall aid was offered to all countries of Europe, but Stalin forbade any Soviet bloc countries to accept it. He knew that the real purpose of Marshall aid was to win friendship for the USA.
- Between 1948 and 1952 the USA gave $13 billion of aid to 16 countries.
- To try to counter the effects of the Marshall Plan, Stalin set up Cominform in 1947 to strengthen co-operation between communists from all countries and Comecon in 1949 to develop economic co-operation between communist countries.

The Berlin blockade and its immediate consequences

- Berlin, like the rest of Germany, had been split into four zones of occupation, but as the city was situated well within the Soviet zone of East Germany, the western zones of Berlin were completely surrounded by communist territory.
- The Western powers wanted to help Germany to recover economically. They believed it was pointless to keep the country in poverty. Stalin wanted to keep Germany weak so that it could not be a threat to the USSR.
- In 1947 Britain and the USA combined their zones of Germany to form 'Bizonia'. They also planned to introduce a new currency, the Deutschmark.
- Stalin opposed these developments, and in June 1948 retaliated by starting a blockade of West Berlin. All road and rail links were cut. West Berlin was cut off from all supplies.
- If the West tried to break the blockade, it could mean war. On the other hand, they could not afford to give in to Stalin.
- The West decided to use an airlift to supply Berlin. Nobody knew at first if this was really possible. It turned out that almost non-stop flights would be needed. Stalin hoped that the airlift would fail. He knew that to fire on the planes would be an act of war.
- The airlift lasted 11 months. There were 275,000 flights made into West Berlin. In May 1949, Stalin gave up and lifted the blockade.
- The victory of the West meant that it could now proceed with its plans for western Germany. The British, French and US zones were united to form the German Federal Republic (West Germany). West Berlin was included in this new country in spite of its location. In August elections were held and the West Germans elected Adenauer as their leader.

- Stalin renamed the Soviet zone the German Democratic Republic (East Germany). This new country came into being in October 1949.
- The Western countries formed NATO (the North Atlantic Treaty Organisation) in 1949. This included most of the democratic Western European countries with the USA and Canada. It was a defensive alliance in which all member countries pledged to assist each other if attacked. Its obvious target was the USSR.
- When NATO was expanded in 1955 to include West Germany, the USSR set up its own military alliance, the Warsaw Pact.

Summary Box 2

The US reaction to Soviet expansion

Truman believed that the spread of communism had to be stopped. This was his policy of 'containment'

The Truman Doctrine (1947) offered help to all countries at risk from communist takeover

The Marshall Plan (1947) gave US financial aid to rebuild the war-torn economies of Western Europe

When Stalin blockaded Berlin in 1948, the Western Allies carried out an 11-month airlift of supplies

When Stalin lifted the blockade in 1949, the western zones of Germany were united to form the German Federal Republic

As a military alliance against Soviet expansion, the Western countries formed NATO in 1949

What do I Know?

1 Name the German philosopher whose writings provide the ideas on which communism is based.
2 What is a 'capitalist'?
3 Which three leaders met at the Yalta Conference?
4 Into how many zones did they agree to split Germany?
5 Which group of Poles did Stalin want to form a new government?
6 Who was the US representative at the Potsdam Conference?
7 Who was the new British Prime Minster who attended the Potsdam Conference?
8 What was the Oder–Neisse Line?
9 What important event happened in Fulton, Missouri on 5 March 1946?
10 Which Czech politician was murdered in 1948?
11 Who was the communist leader of Yugoslavia after the Second World War?

continued

12 Which two countries did Truman aim to save from communist takeover when announcing the Truman Doctrine?

13 Which organisation did Stalin set up in 1947 to strengthen ties between communist parties around the world?

14 What was Bizonia?

15 Name the military alliance formed between communist countries in 1955.

My score …

Using the Sources

Source A

For this topic the only source-based question you might have to answer would be in Section A of Paper 1. Here is an example (remember that in the real examination these questions would have a part (b) too, but it is not source-based).

▼ **A British cartoon of 1947 showing Truman and Stalin as bus drivers competing to take countries to their hotels.**

(a) Study Source A. Explain the message of this cartoon. Support your answer by referring to details of the cartoon and your knowledge. **(6 marks)**

This is one of those cartoons whose meaning is not necessarily immediately obvious. It was drawn in 1947. The cartoonist is commenting on the situation in Europe at that time. It might help you to think of the important things that happened that year, like the Truman Doctrine being announced, as well as the Marshall Plan. In the cartoon Truman and Stalin are competing for business. Stalin seems much more forceful than Truman – he's even pushing people on to his bus. In deciding on your interpretation of the cartoon, take notice of the details: look at the names on the buses (*Pension Russe* means Russian guesthouse), look at the countries which are already on each of the buses. Finally, remember the three steps to gaining full marks on part (a) questions: give your *interpretation* of the cartoon's message, point to *details* of the cartoon which back up your interpretation, and support your answer by explaining features of the cartoon and using *your own knowledge*.

Now have a try at answering question (a) for yourself.

Exam Type Question

Section B of Paper 1 consists of structured questions on the Core Content. Here is an example on the early years of the Cold War in Europe.

> **(a)** What was decided at the Yalta Conference (1945)?
> **(4 marks)**
>
> **(b)** Explain why the USA offered Marshall aid to Europe.
> **(6 marks)**
>
> **(c)** How far do you agree that the Soviet Union was most to blame for the outbreak of the Cold War after 1945? Explain your answer. **(10 marks)**

Have a go yourself at parts (a) and (b), but here are a couple of students' answers to part (c).

Answer 1

The Soviet Union was to blame for the Cold War. Its armies took over eastern Europe at the end of the war and would not allow those countries to decide for themselves what kind of government they wanted. Stalin forced them all to become communist because he wanted the USSR to be protected by a buffer zone against attack from the west, and that's why these countries were called the Iron Curtain. Stalin wanted to spread communism as much as he could. He backed up communists everywhere to take over control, like in Greece, and tried to use Cominform to cause trouble in countries like France and Italy. The West tried its best to get on with Stalin but in the end, as in the case of the Berlin blockade, it was obvious that he could not be trusted.

Answer 2

The Cold War was like any other dispute in that there's usually two sides to any argument. The Russians and the Americans did not trust each other. They always imagined that the other was trying to gain some kind of advantage. For the Russians, the main aim at the end of the war was making sure that the USSR was safe from any future attack. This meant they were determined to keep Germany weak and to dominate eastern Europe. So when their armies liberated a country, they made sure that the new government that was set up was always friendly to the USSR. If necessary, they fixed any elections that were held. In this way the USSR took over pretty well all of eastern Europe. To them it made sense, but to the Americans it looked like the Russians were spreading communism, and denying people democratic rights and freedoms.

It all depends on how you look at it. When Roosevelt was still alive, he got on reasonably well with Stalin. At Yalta, Roosevelt agreed that eastern Europe would be a Soviet sphere of influence. He must have known what this would mean. Yet when Truman became President he started throwing his weight around and demanding that Stalin hold free elections in these countries. This was completely unrealistic. On almost every issue the lack of trust between the two sides meant they would disagree. Look at the Marshall Plan. To the West this was a generous offer by the USA to help rebuild Europe, but to Stalin it was a devious plan by the Americans to win over his communist friends to capitalism. So you cannot really blame the USSR for the Cold War. You could say both sides were to blame for showing little understanding of the other side's point of view, or you could say neither side was to blame because, given the difference in ideology between them, it was impossible to avoid trouble. From the US point of view the Soviets were to blame, but the Soviets would think just the opposite.

Examiner's Comments: Answer 1

6 out of 10

You should know that in part (c) questions the only way you will score the highest marks is to consider *both sides* of the argument. This answer fails to do that. It jumps to the conclusion that the USSR was to blame, and the whole answer focuses on that side of the argument only. It gives a couple of well-explained reasons why.

Answer 2

10 out of 10

This answer avoids the trap of looking at only one side of the argument. In fact, it seems quite reluctant to blame anyone, which is an interesting approach. However, it looks at two or three issues and demonstrates how the lack of trust between the two sides made it impossible for them to agree. It shows that you could blame the USSR for denying freedom in the Iron Curtain countries but it balances this by showing how Truman heightened the tension between the two sides by making unrealistic demands of Stalin. The answer does, then, consider both sides. However, it goes a step further by looking at the issue of *how far* the Soviet Union was to blame, and explaining that the issue of who was to blame is really just a matter of one's perspective. This does everything required for full marks.

1.5 How effectively did the USA contain the spread of communism?

Topic Summary

After 1949 the Cold War continued to develop. In that year, China fell to Mao Zedong's communist forces. The world was divided between the democratic West and the communist East. A nuclear arms race began between the USA and the USSR which threatened the future of the world. A serious crisis over Cuba in 1962 showed how real the danger of nuclear war had become, but the crisis was settled peacefully. During the 1960s the USA attempted to halt the spread of communism in southeast Asia by becoming involved in the Vietnam War. Despite pouring men and resources into South Vietnam, the USA failed to prevent the communists from taking over the country in 1975.

What do I Need to Know?

You will need to be aware of how the Cold War developed between 1949 and 1961. You should be able to explain why and how the Cuban Missile Crisis of 1962 came about, why the USA was able to resolve the crisis successfully, and the significance of these events for the world's future. You will also need to show why the USA felt it necessary to become involved in Vietnam, and why it was unable to win the Vietnam War.

Key Topics

The Cold War, 1949–61

- In 1949 China fell to the communists. This was a serious blow to the USA, but over the years to come China and the USSR failed to work closely together.
- US intervention with UN troops in the Korean War (1950–3) succeeded in preventing South Korea from falling into communist hands.
- The formation of NATO in 1949 and the Warsaw Pact in 1955 divided the world into two hostile alliances – one democratic, the other communist.
- During the 1950s a nuclear arms race between the USA and the USSR started. The development of ICBMs (inter-continental ballistic missiles) meant nuclear warheads could be carried thousands of miles to their targets.
- In 1960 a US U2 spy plane was shot down over the Soviet Union. In protest, the Soviets cancelled a summit meeting with the USA in Paris.

- In 1961 tension rose again over Berlin. The Soviets built the Berlin Wall to prevent East Germans escaping to the West. West Berlin was now totally cut off from the East.

Summary Box 1

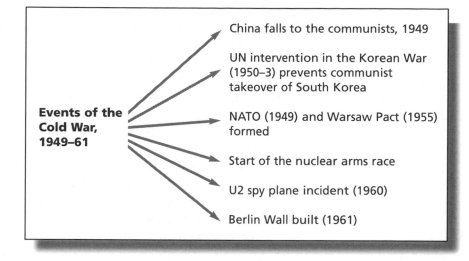

Events of the Cold War, 1949–61

- China falls to the communists, 1949
- UN intervention in the Korean War (1950–3) prevents communist takeover of South Korea
- NATO (1949) and Warsaw Pact (1955) formed
- Start of the nuclear arms race
- U2 spy plane incident (1960)
- Berlin Wall built (1961)

The Cuban missile crisis (1962)

- In 1959 a revolution led by Fidel Castro overthrew the corrupt Cuban dictator, Batista.
- The USA was worried by this as it supported Batista, and it was concerned that Castro would turn out to be a communist.
- When Castro signed a trade treaty with the USSR, the USA banned all trade with the island and, in early 1961, cut off diplomatic relations. It hoped these measures would force Castro out of Russia's influence, but they had the opposite effect.
- In April 1961 the new US President, J. F. Kennedy, supported an attempted invasion of Cuba by Cuban exiles. The invasion force landed at the Bay of Pigs, but was met by much stronger Cuban government forces. The invasion was a dismal failure.
- Castro now turned more to the USSR for help. Khrushchev, the Soviet leader, announced he would give arms to Cuba. Castro nationalised all US-owned businesses in Cuba, and announced he was a communist.
- On 14 October 1962, a US spy plane took pictures which showed missile bases being built in Cuba. If these bases became operational, much of the USA would be brought in range of Soviet missile attack.
- The Americans then discovered that Soviet ships were sailing towards Cuba. On board were missiles for the new bases.
- Kennedy decided to prevent the Soviet ships reaching Cuba. He placed a naval blockade around the island.
- For over a week the world seemed on the brink of nuclear war. Nobody knew what would happen when the Soviet ships reached the US blockade.

- Finally, Khrushchev backed down. He ordered the Soviet ships to turn back.
- But still the crisis was not over. On 26 October 1962 Khrushchev wrote to Kennedy offering to remove the missiles from Cuba if the USA promised not to invade. This was a good offer for Kennedy. But the next day another letter demanded that the USA remove its missiles from Turkey in return for the Soviet missiles being moved from Cuba. To accept this would make Kennedy look weak.
- Kennedy decided to ignore the second letter and reply to the first, accepting the offer. This worked. On 28 October 1962 Khrushchev agreed to dismantle the bases in Cuba.
- The crisis had given the world a serious scare, and both sides took steps to try to avoid any repeat. It was agreed to set up a dedicated telephone link – the 'hot-line' – between Washington and Moscow so that direct communication between the countries' leaders would be possible, and in 1963 a Nuclear Test Ban Treaty was signed.
- The crisis had seriously damaged Khrushchev's prestige. He was the one who finally backed down. In 1964 he was overthrown by his opponents in the USSR.

Summary Box 2

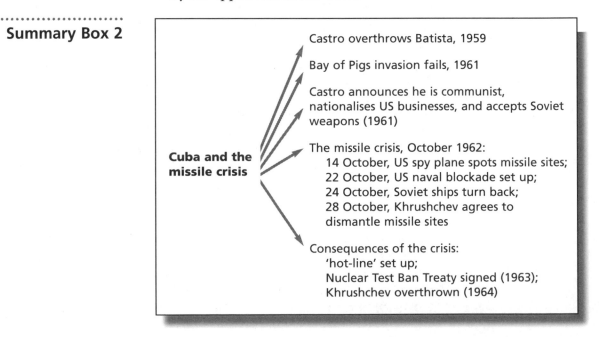

Cuba and the missile crisis

Castro overthrows Batista, 1959

Bay of Pigs invasion fails, 1961

Castro announces he is communist, nationalises US businesses, and accepts Soviet weapons (1961)

The missile crisis, October 1962:
14 October, US spy plane spots missile sites;
22 October, US naval blockade set up;
24 October, Soviet ships turn back;
28 October, Khrushchev agrees to dismantle missile sites

Consequences of the crisis:
'hot-line' set up;
Nuclear Test Ban Treaty signed (1963);
Khrushchev overthrown (1964)

The Vietnam War

- After French colonial rule was overthrown in 1954, Vietnam was divided into two: communist North Vietnam and anti-communist South Vietnam under President Diem.
- Up to 1963 the USA supported Diem's government and gave it aid. The USA was worried about the spread of communism in southeast Asia. The Americans based their policy on the

'domino theory': if they did not stop South Vietnam being taken over by communists, other nations in the area would fall to communism like a row of dominoes.

- The Vietcong, with support from North Vietnam, were fighting to win South Vietnam for communism. From 1961 US servicemen were sent to help South Vietnam combat the Vietcong.
- In 1963 Diem was deposed by army generals. By this time the Vietcong controlled 40 per cent of South Vietnam.
- In 1964 President Johnson used the 'Tonkin Gulf Incident', when North Vietnamese ships attacked a US destroyer in the Gulf of Tonkin, as an excuse to take direct military action in South Vietnam. Soon half a million US troops were in South Vietnam.
- 'Operation Rolling Thunder' – the bombing of North Vietnam – began.
- Although militarily the US troops were much stronger than the Vietcong, they found it impossible to defeat them. The Vietcong used guerrilla tactics. Rarely would they fight in open battle.
- The US troops found it impossible to distinguish between the Vietcong and the general population. Sometimes, as at My Lai in March 1968, US soldiers massacred innocent civilians.
- The USA tried to isolate the Vietcong by putting the rural population into 'strategic villages' – fortified and guarded villages where the population could be protected and supervised. Because the Vietcong hid in the jungle, the USA used 'Agent Orange' and napalm to kill the vegetation.
- The Vietcong built huge underground hideouts and networks of tunnels to protect themselves. Supplies for the Vietcong were sent down the 'Ho Chi Minh trail' from North Vietnam.
- In 1968 the Vietcong launched the Tet Offensive. At first it was successful. Towns and bases all over the country were taken by surprise. Even the US embassy in Saigon was captured. However, the communists had overreached themselves. The USA quickly fought back and inflicted great losses on the Vietcong.
- However, the Tet Offensive did serious damage to US morale. People back in the USA began to think they could not win the war. A protest movement against the war developed.
- Nixon became US President in 1969. He promised to end the war. His solution was 'Vietnamisation' – to get the South Vietnamese to take back control of the war. Obviously the USA would have to give help, but its solders could be withdrawn.
- Peace talks began, and in 1973 a ceasefire was agreed. US troops left Vietnam.
- However, fighting quickly started again, but this time the USA did not get directly involved. In 1975 South Vietnam was overrun by communist troops, and in 1976 it was reunited with North Vietnam.
- Vietnam's neighbours, Laos and Cambodia, also fell into communist hands. The US policy of containment had failed.

Summary Box 3

The Vietnam War

- Vietnam split into North and South Vietnam (1954)
- Vietcong fighting to turn South Vietnam communist
- US supports Diem's government until his overthrow in 1963
- 'Tonkin Gulf Incident' (1964) leads to direct US military involvement
- US bombs North Vietnam
- Vietcong fight guerrilla war against the USA. US casualties increase
- Anti-war movement develops in USA. My Lai massacre and Tet Offensive (1968) increase support for US withdrawal
- Nixon's election leads to eventual US withdrawal by way of the policy of Vietnamisation and peace talks
- US withdrawal in 1973 leaves South Vietnam vulnerable
- Resumption of war in 1974 leads quickly to communist takeover in 1975

What do I Know?

1. In which country did Mao Zedong take power in 1949?
2. Which country was saved from communist takeover by UN intervention in 1950?
3. In which year was the Berlin Wall built?
4. Who was overthrown by Castro in 1959?
5. Which US President supported the 'Bay of Pigs' invasion?
6. How did the USA discover that the USSR was building missile bases in Cuba?
7. What did the USA do to prevent Soviet missiles reaching Cuba?
8. Which Soviet leader was overthrown as a result of the Cuban missile crisis?
9. Which treaty was signed as a consequence of the Cuban missile crisis?
10. Which European country ruled Vietnam until 1954?
11. Name the Communist guerrilla army that was trying to take over South Vietnam.
12. Which South Vietnamese leader was overthrown in 1963?
13. What was 'Operation Rolling Thunder'?
14. Where did an infamous massacre of South Vietnamese villagers take place in March 1968?
15. In which year was Vietnam reunited under communist rule?

My score …

What was the importance of:

- the Bay of Pigs invasion
- the 'hot-line'
- the Ho Chi Minh Trail
- the Tet Offensive?

**Using the
Sources**

For this topic the only source-based question you might have to
answer would be in Section A of Paper 1. Here is an example
(remember that in the real examination these questions would have
a part (b) too, but it is not source-based).

▼ **A British cartoon of 1962 about the Cuban missile crisis.**

Source A

(a) Study Source A. Explain the message of this cartoon. Support
your answer by referring to details of the cartoon and your own
knowledge. **(6 marks)**

First, can you identify the different elements of the cartoon? You
have to recognise the two characters. They are both sitting on
nuclear missiles, and both can press a button which is attached to
their missile. What are they arm-wrestling about? All this should be
clear enough to you. The question is asking you to say what the
message of the cartoon is about the Cuban crisis. Actually it is saying
lots of things, but any interpretation based on details in the cartoon
will do. For example, you might want to make a point about why the
man on the left is sweating, and the man on the right is not. Use your
own knowledge of the Cuban crisis to explain details of the cartoon.

Now have a try at answering question (a) for yourself.

**Exam Type
Question**

Section B of Paper 1 consists of structured questions on the Core
Content. Here is an example on the Vietnam War.

(a) What was the 'Domino Theory'? **(4 marks)**

(b) Explain why the USA introduced the policy of
'Vietnamisation'. **(6 marks)**

(c) How far do you agree that the main reason why the USA
lost the Vietnam War was that the US people stopped
supporting it? Explain your answer. **(10 marks)**

Have a go yourself at parts (a) and (c), but here are a couple of students' answers to part (b).

Answer 1

The policy of Vietnamisation was introduced by President Nixon. The idea was that the USA would train up the Vietnamese to take charge of everything the Americans were doing. The Vietnamese would regain control over the war. The USA would continue to give the South Vietnamese aid, but they would no longer be directly involved.

Answer 2

By the end of the 1960s many Americans believed the USA could not win the Vietnam War. Nixon was looking for a way to get out of Vietnam without giving the impression that the USA had been defeated. He introduced Vietnamisation as a first step to US withdrawal. If a Vietnamese could do a task which an American was doing, then the Vietnamese should do it instead. This applied directly to the conduct of the war. Nixon hoped that if the Vietnamese were given enough help and training, they would be able to run the war successfully themselves. But no matter what happened, Vietnamisation would mean the US could reduce its commitment to South Vietnam, which would mean fewer dead and wounded US soldiers.

Examiner's Comments: Answer 1

3 out of 6

Most part (b) questions ask why events happened. This means the examiners are looking for you to give *reasons* for those events. They will also want you to *explain* those reasons, rather than just identifying them. Explaining a reason means that you can show why it was important, or how it worked. This answer falls short of these requirements. It doesn't give any reason why Vietnamisation was introduced, it just describes Vietnamisation – it says what it was. The examiners will give some marks for this approach, but not many.

Answer 2

5 out of 6

This answer is clearly better than the first. It gives reasons – Nixon wanted to get out of Vietnam; he wanted to reduce the USA's commitment; he wanted to reduce the numbers of US casualties – which are linked together and put in context in a way which serves to explain why the policy was introduced. A bit more background context about what was going on at the time – maybe the influence of the peace movement – would have helped explain why Nixon wanted to withdraw and would have gained full marks.

1.6 How secure was the USSR's control over eastern Europe 1948–c.1989?

Topic Summary

After the Second World War, the Soviet Union's grasp on eastern Europe seemed firm. However, almost from the start people in the Iron Curtain countries showed dissatisfaction at their lack of freedom under communist rule. The first serious resistance to the Soviet Union took place in Hungary in 1956, but this was crushed with great loss of life. In 1968, when Dubcek, a new communist leader, allowed too much freedom in Czechoslovakia the Soviet Union invaded and repressed the reform movement there, though this time with less bloodshed. It was the Polish trade union Solidarity, founded in 1980, that eventually posed the most lasting and serious challenge to Soviet domination. Despite continuous efforts by the Polish communist leadership to crush it, Solidarity survived and became the dominant force in Polish politics. The rapidly declining power of the Soviet Union became clear after Gorbachev came to power in 1985. When he announced that the Soviet Union would no longer interfere in eastern Europe, the communist leaderships in those countries were doomed. During 1989, one after the other, communist countries in eastern Europe were overthrown. The Soviet Union itself was the last casualty. Gorbachev's attempts to reform communism failed, and in December 1991 the Soviet Union was disbanded.

What do I Need to Know?

You need to understand why people in eastern Europe resisted Soviet domination, and how the USSR was, at first, able to repress such opposition. You will have to explain the significance of the rise of Solidarity, both in Poland and for eastern Europe as a whole. The role of Gorbachev in relaxing Soviet control in eastern Europe and in the decline of communism within the Soviet Union must be appreciated, and you will need to judge how much Gorbachev was personally responsible for these events.

Key Topics

Why was there opposition to Soviet control in Hungary in 1956?

- After 1948, Soviet control over eastern Europe seemed secure. Demonstrations in East Germany (1953) and Poland (1956) were easily crushed.

- Stalin's death in 1953 and the emergence of Khrushchev as the new Soviet leader by 1956 gave some hope of a relaxation of Soviet domination in eastern Europe. The appointment in 1956 of Gomulka, who had been imprisoned by Stalin, as leader of the Communist Party in Poland confirmed this trend.
- In 1956, encouraged by these changes, the Hungarians forced their hardline communist leader, Rakosi, to resign. However, his successor, Gero, was equally unpopular.
- By October 1956, Gero seemed to be losing control. There was rioting in Budapest against the government. Members of the secret police, the AVO, were attacked by demonstrators. Soviet tanks were sent into Budapest. Khrushchev approved the appointment of a communist reformer, Nagy, as Prime Minister.
- The Soviet tanks were withdrawn, but Nagy did not act as Khrushchev expected. Instead he announced that Hungary would no longer be a one-party state, and would leave the Warsaw Pact.
- This was a direct threat to Soviet security. On 4 November 1956, 200,000 Soviet troops and 2500 tanks moved against Budapest. The Hungarians fought back.
- Nagy begged for help from the United Nations and the West. He was ignored. The West was involved in the Suez Crisis at the time and had no intention of fighting the USSR over Hungary.
- In two weeks' fighting, over 25,000 Hungarians were killed.
- Soviet control was re-established. Nagy was captured and hanged. He was replaced by a loyal communist, Kadar.

Summary Box 1

Soviet invasion of Hungary, 1956

- Death of Stalin (1953) gives hope of relaxation of Soviet control
- Rakosi, hardline communist leader, overthrown in Hungary, 1956
- Soviet tanks sent in after further rioting in Budapest (October 1956). Nagy made prime minister
- Nagy announces Hungary will withdraw from Warsaw Pact
- Soviet army attacks Budapest, November 1956. In two weeks of fighting, over 25,000 Hungarians die
- Soviet control restored. Nagy executed

Why was there opposition to Soviet control in Czechoslovakia in 1968?

- By 1968, the Soviet Union had a new leader, Brezhnev. He was just as determined as previous leaders to maintain Soviet control of eastern Europe.
- The communist leaders of Czechoslovakia were deeply unpopular with the people. Demonstrations against the low standard of living and lack of freedom were increasing.

- In January 1968, the Communist Party decided to appoint Dubcek as Party Secretary to lead the country. Dubcek was a reformer. He wanted to modernise communism. He talked about 'socialism with a human face'.
- Dubcek gave the people more freedom. Public meetings were allowed. People could criticise the government. The government relaxed its control over industry, and more foreign travel was permitted. These reforms became known as the 'Prague Spring'.
- Dubcek was careful to avoid the mistake the Hungarians had made in 1956. He assured Brezhnev that Czechoslovakia would stay communist and remain in the Warsaw Pact.
- Brezhnev was not fooled. He knew that if the Czechs got more freedom, then other Iron Curtain countries would want the same. Czechoslovakia was too important to the security of the Soviet Union to allow any risks – it was the one country that had a frontier both with West Germany and the USSR.
- Brezhnev warned Dubcek to stop his reforms. The Soviet army was told to carry out 'training exercises' on Czech soil. The final straw for Brezhnev came when Dubcek planned to co-operate with Yugoslavia and Romania, two other countries that showed independent tendencies.
- In August 1968 Warsaw Pact troops took over Czechoslovakia. There was some fighting, but nothing like the bloodshed in Hungary in 1956. The Czechs generally greeted the troops with silent contempt. One student, Jan Palach, burned himself to death in protest.
- Dubcek was arrested and taken to Moscow. He was forced to abandon his reforms. The following year he was thrown out of power and replaced by Husak. A security clampdown in Czechoslovakia saw hundreds of people imprisoned.
- Brezhnev announced that it was the duty of all Warsaw Pact countries to work together to prevent any member abandoning communism. This was the 'Brezhnev Doctrine'.

Summary Box 2

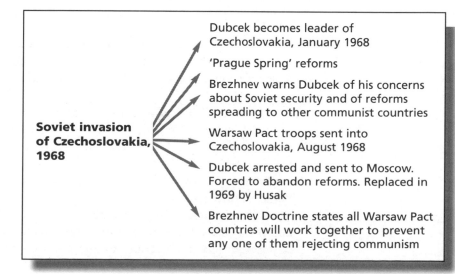

Soviet invasion of Czechoslovakia, 1968

- Dubcek becomes leader of Czechoslovakia, January 1968
- 'Prague Spring' reforms
- Brezhnev warns Dubcek of his concerns about Soviet security and of reforms spreading to other communist countries
- Warsaw Pact troops sent into Czechoslovakia, August 1968
- Dubcek arrested and sent to Moscow. Forced to abandon reforms. Replaced in 1969 by Husak
- Brezhnev Doctrine states all Warsaw Pact countries will work together to prevent any one of them rejecting communism

Why was the Berlin Wall built in 1961?

- After the Second World War, the city of Berlin was split, just like the rest of Germany, into four zones.
- People in communist East Berlin saw people in capitalist West Berlin enjoying a much freer and more prosperous life. A flood of perhaps 2 million people left East Germany for the West between 1949 and 1961. Not only did East Germany lose many skilled people, it was also humiliating for communism that so many wished to leave.
- Khrushchev tried to deal with the problem by threatening the USA and trying to force the West out of Berlin. This did not work, though it made Berlin the focus of Cold War tensions.
- In August 1961 Soviet troops began to construct the Berlin Wall to seal West Berlin off from the East. At first the Wall was no more than barbed wire, but as time passed it became a permanent construction.
- People continued to try to cross the Wall. If detected they would be shot by border guards. In all, 86 people are known to have died in escape attempts. But the Wall did its job. No longer could refugees easily escape to the West.

How important was 'Solidarity'?

- Soviet control was deeply unpopular in Poland. Poles remembered how the Red Army had not helped in the Warsaw Rising of 1944 against the Nazis.
- In the late 1970s the Polish economy was in a poor state. Trade unions were formed and strikers protested against rises in food prices.
- The most popular of the new unions was 'Solidarity', formed in the shipyards of the city of Gdansk (Danzig). Its leader was Lech Walesa. By the end of 1980 it had 9 million members.
- In August 1980 Solidarity called for greater political and religious freedoms. The union was so strong that the government feared to take action against it.
- The Soviet Union became increasingly concerned about Solidarity's influence. However, it had just become involved in war over Afghanistan, and hesitated to take military action against Poland.
- In February 1981 a new Soviet-backed Prime Minister, General Jaruzelski, was appointed. He had orders to deal with Solidarity. In December 1981, he declared martial law, arresting Walesa and many of Solidarity's other leaders. Solidarity was banned. To back Jaruzelski up, the Red Army carried out manoeuvres on Poland's border.
- These tough moves did not work. Solidarity was not crushed and it continued to operate. International pressure led to Walesa being released in 1982, and in 1983 he was awarded the Nobel Peace Prize.

- Over the next few years, Jaruzelski's power dwindled away and Solidarity was the real power in Poland. Once Gorbachev came to power in the Soviet Union, it was only a matter of time before communism collapsed in Poland.

- In 1989 Jaruzelski was forced to agree to free elections. Solidarity won massive support. In 1990 Walesa became President of Poland's first non-communist government in the post-war era.

- Solidarity started as a trade union but quickly developed into the main movement of opposition to communist and Soviet control in Poland. It set an example of resistance to communist control for the rest of eastern Europe.

Summary Box 3

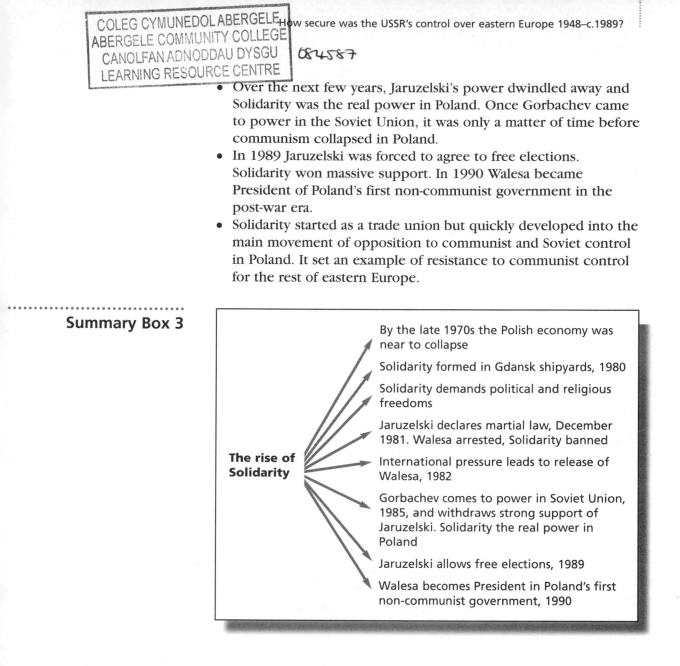

The rise of Solidarity

- By the late 1970s the Polish economy was near to collapse
- Solidarity formed in Gdansk shipyards, 1980
- Solidarity demands political and religious freedoms
- Jaruzelski declares martial law, December 1981. Walesa arrested, Solidarity banned
- International pressure leads to release of Walesa, 1982
- Gorbachev comes to power in Soviet Union, 1985, and withdraws strong support of Jaruzelski. Solidarity the real power in Poland
- Jaruzelski allows free elections, 1989
- Walesa becomes President in Poland's first non-communist government, 1990

How far was Gorbachev responsible for the collapse of Soviet power in eastern Europe?

- By 1985 the Soviet Union was in crisis. Its economy was crumbling, and it was involved in a costly and unwinnable war in Afghanistan.

- In 1985 Gorbachev became leader of the USSR. He planned a programme of reforms to allow the Soviet Union to recover.

- He introduced 'perestroika' (restructuring). This was an attempt to use some capitalist ideas and methods in Soviet industry. Another of his policies was 'glasnost' (openness), meaning that Soviet citizens were allowed to criticise the government.

- Gorbachev also made rapid moves to establish a more friendly relationship with the West. He abandoned the Brezhnev Doctrine and signed arms reduction treaties with the USA.

- Hardline communists could not believe what was going on. Gorbachev seemed to be abandoning all the ideas on which Soviet power was based. In fact, his reforms were introduced too quickly and without proper preparation. The Soviet Union was plunged into confusion and economic chaos.
- For the people of eastern Europe, Gorbachev's reforms signalled that the Soviet Union could no longer dominate their lives.
- During 1989, one by one the communist regimes of eastern Europe toppled and fell, no longer held up by Soviet military power:
  - Hungary – in May 1989 the government opened its border with Austria. The Iron Curtain was breached. In 1990 free elections were held.
  - Poland – in June 1989 Solidarity won free elections. Soon it formed the government with Walesa as President.
  - East Germany – in November 1989 the Berlin Wall was pulled down. Free elections were held in March 1990 which led to the reunification of East and West Germany in October 1990.
  - Czechoslovakia – in November 1989 the 'Velvet Revolution' led to the collapse of the communist government.
  - Bulgaria – in November 1989 the communist dictator Zhirkov resigned and free elections followed in 1990.
  - Romania – in December the communist dictator Ceausescu was overthrown and executed.
- The failure of Gorbachev's reforms and the collapse of communist regimes in eastern Europe led Soviet people to demand an end to communism. Gorbachev's authority disappeared. Communist hardliners attempted a coup in August 1991, but this collapsed.
- Under pressure from Boris Yeltsin, who had emerged as the most popular politician in Russia, Gorbachev signed a decree banning the Communist Party. In December 1991, the Soviet Union itself was disbanded, to be replaced by the short-lived Commonwealth of Independent States (CIS). Gorbachev no longer had a country to lead, and resigned.

Summary Box 4

Gorbachev becomes leader of the USSR, 1985

Gorbachev's reforms – glasnost and perestroika

Gorbachev's foreign policy: peace with the West, arms limitations, Brezhnev Doctrine abandoned

1989, the fall of communist regimes in eastern Europe

Failure of Gorbachev's policies leads to coup attempt by communist hardliners, August 1991

Communist Party in USSR banned. USSR broken up, and Gorbachev resigns, December 1991

Gorbachev and the collapse of communism

What do I Know?

1 Who, by 1956, had replaced Stalin as Soviet leader?

2 In which country was Gomulka appointed leader in 1956?

3 What was the Hungarian secret police called?

4 Who replaced Gero as Hungarian leader in October 1956?

5 In November 1956 the USSR sent tanks into Budapest to prevent Hungary leaving which organisation?

6 The Western powers were unable to intervene in Hungary in 1956 because they were already involved in a crisis elsewhere. Where was this?

7 Which reforming communist became Party Secretary in Czechoslovakia in 1968?

8 Name the student who set fire to himself in protest against the 1968 Soviet invasion of Czechoslovakia.

9 Where in Poland was 'Solidarity' formed?

10 Name the leader of Solidarity who later became President of Poland.

11 Which Polish leader attempted to crush 'Solidarity' in 1981 by imposing martial law?

12 Who became Soviet leader in 1985?

13 What was the policy of 'perestroika'?

14 What Cold War landmark was demolished in November 1989?

15 Which country ceased to exist in December 1991?

My score ...

What was the importance of:

● the Berlin Wall

● the Prague Spring

● the Brezhnev Doctrine

● glasnost?

Using the Sources

For this topic the only source-based question you might have to answer would be in Section A of Paper 1. Here is an example (remember that in the real examination these questions would have a part (b) too, but it is not source-based).

(a) Study Source A on page 54. Explain the message of the cartoon. Support your answer by referring to details of the cartoon and your knowledge. **(6 marks)**

Source A

▲ A British cartoon of October 1956 about events in eastern Europe.

There are a number of features to explain in this cartoon before you deal with its message. You will need to know who the bears' trainer is. The symbol of Russia is the bear, so all these countries are being trained to be like Russian bears. Some are obedient, but some are not. It's significant which bears are disobeying, and it's this that you will need to put into its historical context in order to explain the cartoon's message. Remember what was going on in eastern Europe in 1956 and show how the cartoon comments on these developments. As always with these types of question, remember that there are three elements to the best answers: state what you think the *message* of the cartoon is, indicate features of the cartoon which *back up* your interpretation, and explain these features using your *own knowledge*. Don't imagine that there is only one interpretation of the cartoon. There are many different ways of expressing its message. As long as your interpretation is valid and is properly supported, you'll score the marks.

Now have a try at answering question (a) on page 53 for yourself.

Exam Type Question

Section B of Paper 1 consists of structured questions on the Core Content. Here is an example on the decline and fall of the Soviet Union.

> **(a)** What main problems did Gorbachev face when he became leader of the Soviet Union? **(4 marks)**
>
> **(b)** Why did so many communist regimes in eastern Europe collapse in 1989? **(6 marks)**
>
> **(c)** How far do you agree that Gorbachev was responsible for the collapse of the USSR? Explain your answer.
>
> **(10 marks)**

Have a go yourself at parts (b) and (c), but here are a couple of students' answers to part (a).

Answer 1

The main problems that Gorbachev faced when he became leader of the Soviet Union were that the economy was in big trouble because the quality of industrial goods was so low, that agriculture did not produce enough food for the country, and the war in Afghanistan.

Answer 2

There were many problems Gorbachev faced. The Soviet Union was stuck in a war in Afghanistan that was going badly, and was costing so much that the rest of the economy was suffering from lack of money. Afghanistan was called the 'Soviet Vietnam'. Gorbachev knew that the Soviet economy was in a mess. Industry was inefficient, it did not produce enough consumer goods, and the quality of what it produced was poor. Soviet agriculture could not grow enough food to feed the nation.

Examiner's Comments: Answer 1

3 out of 4

Part (a) questions test your knowledge. You will get a mark for each relevant point, and one additional mark for any extra detail you can give to each point. This means that two points given in good detail will gain the full four marks, so don't waste time by writing too much. On the other hand, you have to provide enough detail so that you don't lose any marks. This answer doesn't quite strike the right balance. It gets the two marks on the economy – one mark for stating that the economy was a problem, and an additional mark for saying what was wrong. However, it merely states the second problem – war in Afghanistan – without expanding it in any way, so only one mark is earned for that point.

Answer 2

4 out of 4

This does the job perfectly. The answer is not too lengthy, so it avoids the trap of wasting time and effort. It makes two clear points – the war and the economy were the problems – and gives some extra detail on each.

2 How was British society changed, 1906–18?

2.1 The reforms of the Liberal governments, 1906–14

Topic Summary

The Liberal government that won the general election of 1906 was responsible for passing a series of social reforms which laid the foundation of a 'welfare state' in Britain. Political and economic changes through the nineteenth century had made Britain more democratic, and produced a growing awareness of the problems of poverty. The work of Booth and Rowntree made it clear that the poor were not to be blamed for poverty. The Liberals passed laws that introduced old age pensions, and National Insurance to protect workers against the effects of illness and unemployment. The state was beginning to take responsibility for helping the poorest and weakest in society.

What do I Need to Know?

You will need to understand the political, social and economic changes of the late nineteenth and early twentieth centuries, which created both a greater awareness of the problems of poverty and a willingness to deal with these problems. You will need to know why some social groups were more at risk of falling into poverty than others, and what measures the Liberal governments took to try to help these groups. You should understand the idea of a 'welfare state' and be able to judge the extent to which the Liberals created a welfare state in Britain before the First World War.

Key Topics

Why did the Liberal governments introduce welfare reforms?

The young, old and unemployed

1 Political changes

- The Reform Acts of 1867 and 1884 gave the vote (the 'franchise') to many working-class men. By 1900 about half the electorate came from the working classes. Both main political parties, the Liberals and the Conservatives, wanted to attract support from the working classes.
- The emergence of a 'Labour' Party after 1900 gave working people a party to represent their interests. A Labour Representation Committee was set up in 1900 to help 'Labour' candidates in Parliamentary elections. So by 1900 political developments meant that priority could be given to the needs of working-class people.

2 Social and economic changes

- The Industrial Revolution transformed Britain. The new industrial towns created many social problems such as poor working conditions, poor housing and overcrowding, and public health problems.
- Governments began to pass laws, such as Factory Acts, Public Health Acts and Education Acts, to protect people against the effects of these social and economic changes.
- After 1906 the Liberals took this idea further by passing laws to try to guarantee a basic standard of living for all.

3 Outstanding political personalities

- The Liberal governments had many outstanding ministers who were prepared to fight for better social conditions, such as Lloyd George, Chancellor of the Exchequer from 1908, and Winston Churchill.

4 Poverty and the Poor Law

- The poor in the nineteenth century could get help from their parish, but this help was limited by principles laid down in the Poor Law of 1834.
- The able-bodied poor had to agree to go into a workhouse, where conditions were hard. Only the desperate would do this.
- In some industrial areas the Poor Law broke down because there was so much unemployment that workhouses could not cope with all the poor. Here 'outdoor relief' – handouts of money or food – had to be given. People began to realise that a better way to deal with poverty was needed.

5 Booth and Rowntree

- Towards the end of the nineteenth century attitudes towards the poor began to change. Instead of blaming the poor for their own poverty, several writers studied the lives of the poor and demonstrated how poverty was caused.
- The most famous of these writers were Charles Booth, who wrote *Life and Labour of the People in London* between 1886 and 1903, and Seebohm Rowntree, who wrote *Poverty: A Study of Town Life* in 1901 about the city of York.
- Both writers found that an income of £1 a week was the minimum needed to keep a family of five above the 'poverty line'. They discovered about 30 per cent of the population living below the poverty line, and identified sickness, old age, unemployment, low wages and large families as the main causes of poverty.

Summary Box 1

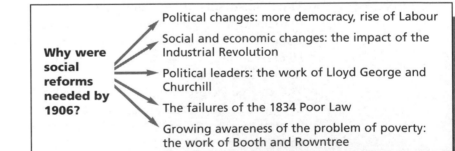

Why were social reforms needed by 1906?

- Political changes: more democracy, rise of Labour
- Social and economic changes: the impact of the Industrial Revolution
- Political leaders: the work of Lloyd George and Churchill
- The failures of the 1834 Poor Law
- Growing awareness of the problem of poverty: the work of Booth and Rowntree

How effective were the Liberal reforms?

- **Children:** the School Meals Act (1906) provided free school meals for the poor. Free school medical checks were introduced in 1907. The 'Children's Charter' was passed in 1908; it included measures to deal with young offenders, limited working hours for children, and set up Child Care Committees to tackle cases of neglect.

- **Old age pensions:** old age was the single most important cause of poverty. The Old Age Pensions Act (1908) introduced pensions from 1909 for the poorest people over the age of 70. The pension was 5s (shillings) a week, payable to those with an income of less than £21 a year. Smaller pensions were paid to those who were slightly better off. Pensions were collected from the Post Office and were paid for out of taxation. Opponents argued it would discourage people from saving for their retirement and make people dependent on government handouts. In fact, it transformed life for a million pensioners by 1913.

- **Labour Exchanges:** Labour Exchanges were the idea of the economist William Beveridge. The Labour Exchanges Act (1909) was passed to help the unemployed find work. Labour Exchanges were set up all over the country. The unemployed had to register with their local exchange to receive their National Insurance benefit payments, and local employers would notify the exchange of job vacancies.

- **Low pay:** the Trade Boards Act (1909) tried to improve pay and working conditions in small-scale industries not covered by the rules of the Factory Acts. Minimum pay rates were set for these industries.

- **National Insurance:** the National Insurance Act (1911) was in two parts; one dealing with sickness and the other with unemployment. Lloyd George introduced a system of health insurance by which all workers earning £160 a year or less paid 4d (pence) a week into a fund. Their employer added 3d and the government 2d. Employers ran the scheme which gave workers free medical care and sickness benefit for 26 weeks. Churchill was responsible for the scheme of unemployment insurance. This covered only trades particularly at risk from seasonal unemployment, such as building and engineering. Workers paid 2.5d a week, and this was matched by the employer. When unemployed, workers received 7s a week for up to 15 weeks, not a living wage, but some relief from the effects of being out of work.

Summary Box 2

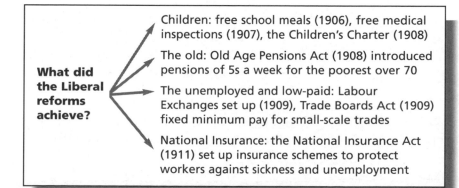

What did the Liberal reforms achieve?

Children: free school meals (1906), free medical inspections (1907), the Children's Charter (1908)

The old: Old Age Pensions Act (1908) introduced pensions of 5s a week for the poorest over 70

The unemployed and low-paid: Labour Exchanges set up (1909), Trade Boards Act (1909) fixed minimum pay for small-scale trades

National Insurance: the National Insurance Act (1911) set up insurance schemes to protect workers against sickness and unemployment

The significance of the Liberal reforms

- Many wealthy and middle-class people opposed the reforms. They were outraged by Lloyd George's 'People's Budget' of 1909 which raised taxes. They resented paying for the reforms out of taxation. They claimed that handouts would make the poor lazy and dependent on the state.
- In fact, the Liberal reforms were quite modest in their effects. There was little redistribution of income from the rich to the poor.
- Most of the reforms were paid for by those who were in work. The insurance principle meant that workers who received benefits had paid for them.
- Despite these reservations, the Liberals were certainly prepared to go further than any previous government in using the resources of the state to intervene in people's lives. They did not create a welfare state, but they certainly provided the foundations of one.

What do I Know?

1 What is the franchise?
2 To which social group was the franchise extended by the Reform Acts of 1867 and 1884?
3 Which were the two main political parties in Britain at the start of the twentieth century?
4 What was the purpose of the Labour Representation Committee, set up in 1900?
5 Who became Chancellor of the Exchequer in 1908?
6 What was *outdoor relief* under the 1834 Poor Law?
7 What was the single most important cause of poverty in the early twentieth century?
8 Who wrote *Life and Labour of the People in London*?
9 In which city did Seebohm Rowntree do the research for *Poverty: A Study of Town Life*?
10 What help did the government give to children of the poor from 1906?
11 How old did you have to be to qualify for an old age pension in 1909?
12 How poor did you have to be to qualify for the maximum old age pension?
13 Who thought up the idea of Labour Exchanges?
14 Why could the government claim that workers were getting 'nine pence for four pence' out of the health insurance scheme?
15 Where did the unemployed have to register to receive unemployment insurance benefits?

My score …

What was the importance of:
- the 1834 Poor Law
- the Poverty Line
- the Children's Charter
- the People's Budget, 1909?

Exam Type Question

The Britain Depth Study is tested only in Paper 2. This paper is a source-based investigation of an issue taken from the Depth Study. There will be between five and seven questions to answer on a range of source material. All the questions are compulsory. The questions will require you to interpret and evaluate the sources (Assessment Objective 2), and to show that you are aware of how events are interpreted and represented in different ways (Assessment Objective 3). However, this doesn't mean that your own knowledge of the topic (Assessment Objective 1) is unimportant. Many of the questions will expect you to use your knowledge to help you make sense of the sources, and to make judgements on their reliability and utility.

Take a look at this question. Have a go at answering it, and then consider your answer in the light of the examples and comments that follow.

Source A

▼ A Conservative Party election poster of 1910. The Conservatives wanted to tax foreign trade rather than raise income tax.

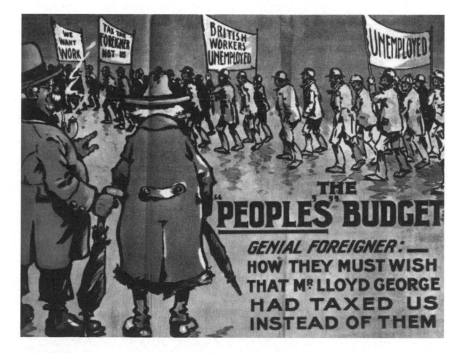

(a) Study Source A. Do you think this poster gives a reliable impression of the impact of the 'People's Budget'? Support your answer by referring to details of the cartoon and your knowledge. **(8 marks)**

Many questions on sources deal with the issue of reliability. They are really asking whether or not you can trust what the source tells you. One of the most serious errors you can make in answering these questions is to think that making general comments about *types* of sources will do. A weak student would look at Source A and say that it is not reliable because it is a cartoon, or because cartoons are supposed to make people laugh, or because cartoonists are biased, and so on. Such answers *ignore* the content of the source – what it actually shows. Without judging the reliability of the content, you will not get anywhere.

The details of a source will often get you thinking about reliability. Is the language used suspicious – is it over-emotional or extreme in some way? Or, if the source is a picture, does it make fun of some of the characters or show them in an unflattering way? These kinds of details can be an indication of a particular opinion or point of view. They can show that the source is one-sided, or biased.

One of the best ways of working out whether you can trust a source is to *check* its content against other information you have. In the examination paper there will be several sources, and you could check a source against one or more of the others. If they agree, it might mean that you can believe them all – but be careful, there could be other reasons for the agreement. If they disagree, you can consider possible reasons why this is so. This kind of checking is called *cross-referencing*. You can also cross-reference what a source says against your own knowledge of the topic. If you know something which proves the reliability (or unreliability) of a source, then say so! In fact, this is one of the most important ways, in Paper 2, of demonstrating your own knowledge of the topic.

Lastly, you can get clues about reliability by considering the *purpose* of the person who created the source. Why did the artist draw this particular poster? And what about the *audience* for whom it was drawn? By explaining why the artist represented the People's Budget in this way, you will also be commenting on the poster's reliability as a piece of evidence.

Answer 1

There's no chance that this source gives a reliable opinion on the People's Budget because it's a Conservative election poster. You can be sure the Conservatives would have criticised Lloyd George just because he was a Liberal and was a political opponent of the Conservatives. You can see that's exactly what they do: they show all the workers out of work because of the Budget.

Answer 2

> Source A shows that loads of people have been made unemployed because of Lloyd George's People's Budget. It's saying that British workers would have preferred the Conservatives to put up taxes on trade, rather than pay for the Liberals' reforms through income tax. This isn't true, though. The amount of extra tax people had to pay was very small because most of the reforms were paid for by insurance schemes. This poster wasn't printed to tell the truth about the People's Budget, because it's an election poster. It's trying to persuade people that Lloyd George was doing a bad job and that they should vote for the Conservatives instead. That's why the Conservatives show the picture in this way, because it's their point of view, probably because they were the rich people and they didn't want to pay more tax.

Examiner's Comments: Answer 1

4 out of 8

This answer is rather short, but it has some valid points. First, it does use the content of the source to illustrate the point that the Conservatives were bound to be hostile to the People's Budget. Although it mentions the fact that the source is an election poster, it doesn't *develop* any points about the source's *purpose*. It simply makes the point that the Conservatives were bound to give an unreliable opinion about the Budget, and explains this using the fact that the Conservatives were political opponents of the Liberals. In other words, the answer detects and illustrates the bias in the source, and explains this bias using background knowledge.

Answer 2

8 out of 8

This is a much more sophisticated answer. First, it shows detailed contextual knowledge by demonstrating that the content of the source is unreliable in what it says about the impact of the People's Budget. This student knows that the Liberal reforms involved relatively little redistribution of wealth from the rich to the poor through increased taxation. Why, then, does the poster pretend that the impact was harmful? The answer goes on to explain the purpose of the poster – that it's trying to win votes by persuading people that Lloyd George was doing a bad job. Finally, it places this in context by noting that the rich opposed the People's Budget because they didn't want to pay more tax. This answer displays the skills which examiners look for in answering questions on the reliability of sources – cross-reference and explanation of purpose using contextual knowledge.

2.2   The Suffragettes and Votes for Women

Topic Summary

In the nineteenth century, men and women were not equal. Society was dominated by men. However, by 1900, this was beginning to change. Greater opportunities at work and in education were opening up for women. A women's movement, demanding equal rights, had begun. One issue in particular – the right to vote – became the focus of their campaign. Moderate women supported the Suffragists, who believed in peaceful tactics. However, in 1903, a more militant group emerged. These were the Suffragettes, led by Emmeline Pankhurst. They used more violent methods to achieve their goal: smashing windows, assaulting politicians, and even arson. At the 1913 Derby, a suffragette called Emily Davison ran in front of the horses and was killed. Suffragettes who had been imprisoned went on hunger strike and had to be force-fed. The Suffragettes' campaign ended only when the First World War broke out in 1914.

What do I Need to Know?

You will need to know why women's rights were emerging as a major issue by the end of the nineteenth century, and what the arguments were both for and against female suffrage. You will need to understand why the Suffragettes' campaign made such an impact, and why the authorities found it so difficult to deal with the women. You will also need to judge whether the women's campaign helped their cause, or whether the use of violence hindered it by alienating potential supporters.

Key Topics

What were the arguments for and against women's suffrage?

- In the nineteenth century women had fewer rights than men.
- By 1900 attitudes were changing. More women were getting a good education, going out to work and living independent lives. Inventions like the telephone and typewriter opened up new types of work to women. Teaching was the main profession for educated women. However, up until the First World War, barely 10 per cent of married women went out to work.
- A movement for women's rights developed. It focused on winning the right to vote.

ARGUMENTS AGAINST WOMEN'S SUFFRAGE	ARGUMENTS FOR WOMEN'S SUFFRAGE
• Politics was for men. Women would not understand political issues. • Many women, like Queen Victoria, were against votes for women. • Only middle-class women wanted the vote. Other women felt there were much more important social issues to fight for. • Not all men could vote, so why should women? • Nobody planned to give the vote to all women. But even if only some got the vote, the political effects were not clear. • The violent tactics of some campaigners for women's rights showed they did not deserve the vote. • Women could not fight in war, so they should not be involved in making national decisions.	• Women had as much right to vote as men. • Votes for women had already been introduced in other parts of the world such as New Zealand and Australia. • Some women were allowed to vote in local elections. Why not elections for parliament too? • Women were becoming more educated and independent. • It would be democratic to give women the vote. In the nineteenth century more men were given the vote, so now was the time to include women.

How effective were the activities of the Suffragists and the Suffragettes?

- In 1897 Millicent Fawcett founded the National Union of Women's Suffrage Societies (NUWSS). This was a moderate and peaceful organisation which campaigned for votes for women. Its members were called Suffragists. It won much support but more radical groups lost patience with its approach and the slow pace of change that resulted.
- In 1903 Emmeline Pankhurst and her daughter Christabel founded the Women's Social and Political Union (WSPU). Another daughter, Sylvia, worked in the East End of London, trying to improve social conditions for working-class women. She quarreled with her mother and sister, and started her own organisation, the Women's Suffrage Federation.
- The WSPU, who became known as the Suffragettes, believed in taking action to bring the campaign for women's suffrage into the public eye. They staged demonstrations, disturbed the meetings of political opponents and chained themselves to railings in public places. These unfeminine tactics astonished most people.
- As time passed, the Suffragettes' tactics became increasingly violent and were often illegal. Many were arrested for smashing windows, as in the famous London demonstration of March 1912, as well as assaulting politicians and arson. Parliament debated votes for women several times, but even sympathetic MPs were put off by the Suffragettes' violence.

- During the 1913 Derby, a Suffragette, Emily Davison, walked out in front of the horses and was killed. It was clear that she intended to stage a demonstration, but she was treated by the Suffragette movement as a martyr.
- The authorities did not know how to deal with the Suffragettes. Many Suffragettes came from comfortable, middle-class backgrounds and most men could not see what they had to complain about.
- As the violence increased, more and more Suffragettes were sent to jail where many went on hunger strike. The authorities responded by force-feeding them, which caused an outcry. The government then passed the 'Cat and Mouse' Act, by which hunger strikers were released from prison, but re-arrested once their health improved. Emmeline Pankhurst was arrested and re-arrested six times during 1913.
- When the First World War broke out in August 1914, the Suffragettes abandoned their campaign and supported the war effort. It was the contribution women made during the war that led directly to votes for some women being won in 1918.
- It is impossible to know whether the Suffragettes' campaign would eventually have worked. Their supporters insist that without their efforts men would never have accepted votes for women. Their opponents argue that the violence of the Suffragettes did more harm than good by making it impossible for men who accepted the justice of their cause to support them.

Summary Box 1

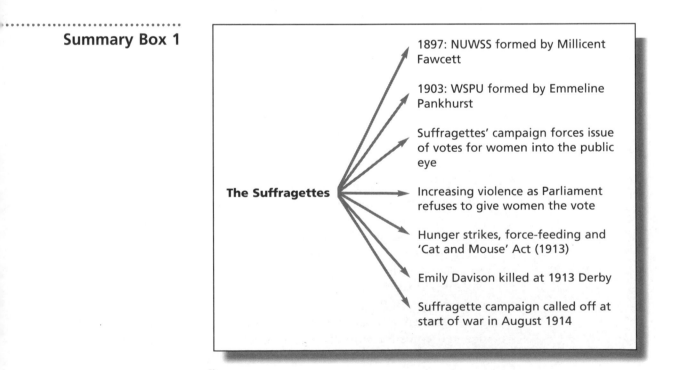

The Suffragettes

1897: NUWSS formed by Millicent Fawcett

1903: WSPU formed by Emmeline Pankhurst

Suffragettes' campaign forces issue of votes for women into the public eye

Increasing violence as Parliament refuses to give women the vote

Hunger strikes, force-feeding and 'Cat and Mouse' Act (1913)

Emily Davison killed at 1913 Derby

Suffragette campaign called off at start of war in August 1914

What do I Know?

1 What proportion of married women went out to work in the years just before the First World War?

2 Name one nineteenth-century invention that produced job opportunities in offices for women.

3 In the early twentieth century, what was the profession that was most open to educated women?

4 What was Queen Victoria's attitude towards votes for women?

5 Name one country that gave votes to women before Britain.

6 Who was the leader of the NUWSS?

7 What were members of the NUWSS known as?

8 Name Emmeline Pankhurst's two daughters who were involved in the movement for votes for women.

9 What kind of demonstration did the Suffragettes stage in London at the beginning of March 1912?

10 At which event was Emily Davison killed in June 1913?

11 How was she killed?

12 How did prison authorities at first react to Suffragettes going on hunger strike?

13 What act was passed because of the hunger strikes?

14 Who was arrested and re-arrested six times during 1913?

15 How did the Suffragettes react to the outbreak of the First World War?

My score ...

What was the importance of:
- the Suffragists
- the WSPU
- the 'Cat and Mouse' Act of 1913
- the 1913 Derby?

Exam Type Question

The Britain Depth Study is tested only in Paper 2. This paper is a source-based investigation of an issue taken from the Depth Study. There will be between five and seven questions to answer on a range of source material. All the questions are compulsory. The questions will require you to *interpret* and *evaluate* the sources (Assessment Objective 2), and to show that you are aware of how events are interpreted and represented in *different ways* (Assessment Objective 3). However, this doesn't mean that your own knowledge of the topic (Assessment Objective 1) is unimportant. Many of the questions will expect you to use your knowledge to help you make sense of the sources and to make judgements on their reliability and utility, or, as in the following example, to explain the context in which a particular source was produced.

Take a look at question (a) on page 68. Have a go at answering it, and then consider your answer in the light of the examples and comments which follow.

Source A

THE SHRIEKING SISTER.

The Sensible Woman. "*YOU* HELP OUR CAUSE? WHY, YOU'RE ITS WORST ENEMY!"

▲ **A cartoon of 1906 from the magazine 'Punch'.**

(a) Study Source A. Why do you think this cartoon was published in 1906? Support your answer by referring to details of the cartoon and your own knowledge. **(6 marks)**

There's a question within a question here, and the best answers will understand that they have to deal with both aspects: first, why was the cartoon published and, second, why in 1906? It would be possible to answer dealing with only one of these aspects but, if you do this, you won't score very highly. Good answers will be built on a sound interpretation of the cartoon. This means identifying the cartoonist's message and, as the question demands, using details of the cartoon to support your interpretation. Once you have done this you will need to explain why this message was particularly relevant *in 1906*, which means using your knowledge of what was happening at the time.

Answer 1

> I think this cartoon was published because 1906 was the time when the Suffragettes started causing all their disruption, like smashing windows and chaining themselves to railings. That's why the cartoonist thought it would be a good idea to do a cartoon about them.

Answer 2

> The cartoonist probably is quite in favour of votes for women because the cartoon seems to show that he or she is worried that the violence of the Suffragettes will do more harm than good. You can see this because the sensible woman talks about 'our cause', meaning that she wants the vote but that she knows the violence will just put everyone off. This cartoon would have been published in 1906 because this is about the time when the public began to take notice of the Suffragettes. The Suffragettes were only started in 1903. By 1906 they were doing things like shouting out in public meetings and chaining themselves to park railings. So the cartoonist is warning that these tactics won't work.

Examiner's Comments: Answer 1

1 out of 6

This answer gives a reason why the cartoon was published *in 1906* but manages to do this without making any direct reference to its message. This cannot, then, be a complete answer because it would apply equally to *any* cartoon about the Suffragettes from 1906. The question asks why this cartoon in particular was produced at that time. The question includes a specific instruction to support your answer using details of the cartoon, and ignoring such instructions will almost always carry a heavy penalty.

Answer 2

6 out of 6

This answer is very methodical. First it identifies the cartoon's message – that the violence will do more harm than good. At the end of the answer it takes the message a stage further and states the cartoonist's *purpose* – to give a warning against the violent tactics. These points are backed up by details of the cartoon, as required. Finally, there is a specific section of the answer that uses contextual knowledge to explain why the cartoon's message was relevant to 1906. This is a good example of how a relatively brief answer can still provide all that is required.

2.3 British society and the First World War

Topic Summary

When war broke out in August 1914, men rushed to join the armed forces. Everyone thought the war would be over quickly, but they were wrong. Once it became clear that the war would be a long one, British society had to make great changes to support the war effort. The government, through the Defence of the Realm Act, gave itself greater powers over people's lives than ever before. In 1916 conscription was introduced, and from 1917 food rationing was necessary. In order to ensure public support for the war effort, the government made widespread use of propaganda. Women made a great contribution to winning the war – filling the jobs that soldiers left behind and taking on a range of work that previously would have been closed to them. By the end of the war almost everyone agreed that women had earned the right to vote, and this was given to some women in the Representation of the People Act of 1918. The war created much bitterness among the British people. When the Paris Peace Conference met in 1919, they wanted revenge against Germany.

What do I Need to Know?

You will need to understand the impact that the First World War had on British society and on civilian life. You will need to know how the government took ever greater control over people's lives in order to ensure that the war effort was successful. You should understand how the government used propaganda to shape public opinion. You should know about the contribution women made to the war effort, and understand why they were given the vote in 1918. You will need to know what the attitude of the British people was towards Germany by the end of the war, and how this influenced the peacemakers at the Paris Peace Conference.

Key Topics

How were civilians affected by the war?

- At the start of the war, volunteers rushed to join up. Lord Kitchener, Minister of War, was in charge of recruiting men for the armed forces. Half a million men enlisted in the first six weeks of the war. Everyone expected the war to be over by Christmas.
- When the war dragged on and casualties began to rise, the early enthusiasm disappeared. A massive propaganda campaign was needed to keep up the numbers of new volunteers.

- The government was reluctant to introduce conscription (compulsory military service) as this had never been done before, but by 1916 there was no choice. The numbers volunteering had dwindled and losses in the fighting were great. The 'Derby Scheme', which had asked men to pledge themselves to join up if they were needed, had been a failure. The Military Service Acts (1916) brought in conscription, first for unmarried men and then for all men aged between 18 and 41. Around 16,000 conscientious objectors refused to fight. Most of these accepted other war work, but around 1500 refused any co-operation and were imprisoned.

- The Defence of the Realm Acts (DORA) of 1914 gave the government wide powers to take any actions necessary for winning the war. The government took over all the mass media, ordered workers to stay in vital jobs, took over mines and railways, introduced British Summer Time, and watered down beer. Almost no area of life was out of the reach of DORA.

- German submarine attacks sank many of the ships that were bringing food to Britain and by 1917 there were food shortages. DORA allowed the government to take over land to grow food. It also set up the 'Land Army' in which women could join up for agricultural work.

- In 1917 sugar rationing began. Households were given ration cards that entitled each one to half a pound of sugar a week. In 1918 rationing was extended to meat, tea and butter. Strangely, despite food shortages, many of the poor had an improved diet because of the higher wages they could earn during the war.

Summary Box 1

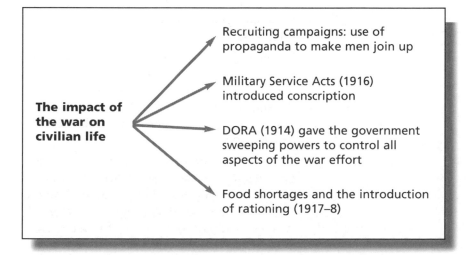

The impact of the war on civilian life

Recruiting campaigns: use of propaganda to make men join up

Military Service Acts (1916) introduced conscription

DORA (1914) gave the government sweeping powers to control all aspects of the war effort

Food shortages and the introduction of rationing (1917–8)

How effective was government propaganda during the war?

- Propaganda was required to ensure a positive public attitude towards the war effort. People needed to feel they were fighting a 'just war'. Often this meant encouraging extreme anti-German views.

- Atrocity stories about the German armed forces were common. Many of these stories were false or exaggerated.

- DORA gave the government control over the mass media, but most newspaper editors saw it as their patriotic duty to support the war effort, and so they made sure that reports on the war were always positive. Much propaganda was produced by private companies.

- Propaganda was not just about stirring up anti-German feelings. Government campaigns also focused on issues like saving food, investing in war savings, or working in vital industries.

- Early in the war the government set up a Propaganda Bureau. Later this developed into the Department of Information which co-ordinated propaganda efforts. In March 1918 this became the Ministry of Information headed by Lord Beaverbrook.

How did women contribute to the war effort?

- When the war started in 1914, the Suffragettes immediately abandoned their campaign for the vote and promised to support the war.

- By 1915 government efforts to get women involved in war work had been so slow that the Suffragettes organised a demonstration demanding the 'Right to Serve'. From this time on, the numbers of women involved in war work increased rapidly.

- Women took on all kinds of work previously regarded as suitable for men only. They became drivers, bus conductors, police, railway workers, engineering workers, munitions workers (many of whom were known as 'canaries' as the explosives turned their skin yellow) – any work vacated by men joining the armed forces.

- For many women, particularly from the middle classes, the war provided their first experience of the world of work. All women experienced a sense of greater independence and were aware of the importance of their efforts in winning the war. Never again could there be such sharp divisions between men's and women's work.

- Towards the end of the war, parliament began to consider changes to the franchise. Before the war not even all men had the vote. It was clear that this would be changed, so why not include women too? Through their work during the war, women had won over most of those men who had opposed the Suffragettes before the war.

- In the Representation of the People Act (1918) all men over the age of 21 were given the vote. Women over the age of 30 who were householders or wives of householders were also given the vote. This was still discrimination against women, but everyone knew it was just a first step and that equal voting rights would soon follow. This took another 10 years: in 1928 all women over 21 got the vote.

Summary Box 2

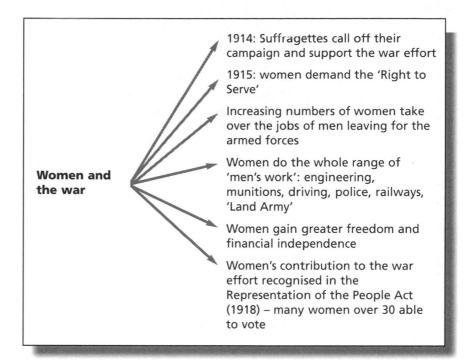

Women and the war

1914: Suffragettes call off their campaign and support the war effort

1915: women demand the 'Right to Serve'

Increasing numbers of women take over the jobs of men leaving for the armed forces

Women do the whole range of 'men's work': engineering, munitions, driving, police, railways, 'Land Army'

Women gain greater freedom and financial independence

Women's contribution to the war effort recognised in the Representation of the People Act (1918) – many women over 30 able to vote

British attitudes towards Germany and the Paris Peace Conference

- Casualties in the war had been so numerous that few families escaped bereavement. By the end of the war most people in Britain wanted revenge on Germany. They wanted to 'Hang the Kaiser'.
- Anti-German feelings throughout the war had been whipped up by propaganda. Germans were seen as brutes and barbarians.
- The British general election of 1918 made matters worse. The candidates were under pressure to make Germany pay. Even Lloyd George, the Prime Minister, was guilty of promising a harsh and punitive peace on Germany. At an election meeting in Bristol, he said, 'Germany must pay to the uttermost farthing, and we shall search their pockets for it.'
- The effect of the anti-German atmosphere was to make it hard for the peacemakers, who assembled in Paris in 1919, to agree a fair and balanced peace, even though many of them realised that a harsh treaty would simply make Germany resentful and store up trouble for the future.

What do I Know?

1 How did the Suffragettes react to the outbreak of the First World War?
2 Why did women have to demand the 'Right to Serve' in 1915?
3 What organisation did women who wanted to work in agriculture join?

continued

4 Why did the skin of some munitions workers turn yellow?

5 At the start of the war, who was in charge of recruiting men for the armed forces?

6 What did the initials DORA stand for?

7 What was the 'Derby Scheme'?

8 Which acts introduced conscription in 1916?

9 What were those people who refused to fight called?

10 Why did food become in short supply in 1917?

11 What was the first food to be rationed?

12 Who was in charge of the Ministry of Information, set up in 1918?

13 Which women were given the vote in 1918?

14 By the end of the war, what did most British people want to do to the German Kaiser?

15 In an election meeting in Bristol in 1918, what did Lloyd George promise to do to Germany?

My score …

What was the importance of:

- DORA
- conscription
- conscientious objectors
- the Representation of the People Act, 1918?

Exam Type Question

The Britain Depth Study is tested only in Paper 2. This paper is a source-based investigation of an issue taken from the Depth Study. There will be between five and seven questions to answer on a range of source material. All the questions are compulsory. The questions will require you to *interpret* and *evaluate* the sources (Assessment Objective 2), and to show that you are aware of how events are interpreted and represented in *different ways* (Assessment Objective 3). However, this doesn't mean that your own knowledge of the topic (Assessment Objective 1) is unimportant. Many of the questions will expect you to use your knowledge to help you make sense of the sources and to make judgements on their reliability and utility, or, as in the following example, to explain the context in which a particular source was produced.

Take a look at this question. Have a go at answering it, and then consider your answer in the light of the examples and comments which follow.

(a) Study Source A on page 75. How useful do you think this picture would be as evidence about women's role in the First World War? Support your answer by referring to the picture and your own knowledge. **(6 marks)**

Questions that deal with the *usefulness*, or utility, of sources are often asked on Paper 2. Basic answers to such questions simply state that the source is useful for the information it provides. This is, of course, true, but it's only part of the story, not least because the question asks '*how* useful?' In other words, you are asked not just to consider the ways in which the source is useful, but also to think about its limitations. So slightly better answers will first say what the source shows, and then say that this is of limited use because there are other things about the topic that the source does not show. So far the answer might just have earned half marks. What's missing is any *evaluation* of the source – any sense of questioning whether what the source says can be trusted or not. Clearly, if you cannot believe a source, then it can't be useful. Or rather, it can still be useful, but in a different way – not as factual information, but perhaps as evidence of why someone might wish to mislead or misrepresent events. With Source A, for example, the fact that it was painted by an official artist might make a difference to how you use the source. You should at least consider the possibility that the government might wish women's work to be portrayed in a certain light, perhaps to give a particular message or image to the viewer. This is where your knowledge of the topic can come in, to help you judge whether or not the picture is factually accurate. The highest marks in utility questions will always go to answers which don't just take the source at face value, but which use source evaluation to judge its usefulness.

Source A

▼ A painting from 1917 showing women munitions workers. It was painted by an official government artist whose task was to paint pictures of various aspects of the war.

Answer 1

I think this painting is extremely useful in telling us about the role of women in the war because it shows women working in a munitions factory. You can see all the types of work they did, like working on machines and stuffing explosive into shells. You can get a good idea of how dangerous the work must have been. You can also see how orderly and proud the women were. You can see them working hard and there's a good spirit. Of course, there are things about women's work the picture does not show. They did lots of other things apart from working in munitions factories, like the Land Army and being bus conductors. In fact they did all the jobs that men could no longer do once they had gone into the army. This picture doesn't show any of those things, but I still think it's pretty useful.

Answer 2

This source is useful about women and the war but you have to be a bit careful with it. Because it's an official picture, the artist sets out to represent the women in a certain way. The artist wants the viewer to sympathise with the women, and to admire them. You can tell by the way the picture focuses on the girl in the middle. She's a typical, hardworking person, and she's putting her life in danger by carrying around the explosives. The artist makes her like a symbol for all women's contribution to the war effort. This doesn't mean the picture is completely unreliable. Women did work in munitions factories and they did do all the kinds of work you can see. But in a way the picture is much more useful as evidence of the kind of image the government wanted to promote of women workers than as evidence of the work itself.

Examiner's Comments: Answer 1

3 out of 6

This is actually a detailed and careful answer. It picks out several details in the picture and shows how they are useful as evidence about women's work in the war. It then uses background knowledge to show that there are things about women's work that the source does not show. The problem is that the answer is uncritical. It accepts the picture as the literal truth about women working in munitions factories. There is no attempt to evaluate the source. This is a serious limitation.

Answer 2

6 out of 6

This answer is based on a real understanding of the nature of the particular source. It starts from the idea that the artist may have a purpose in representing the women in this way, and that he or she sets out to create an image for the viewer. The subtlety in the answer is that the writer knows this does *not* make the picture unreliable. It does give information about women's work which is accurate, but much more interestingly it provides evidence of how official artists shaped public opinion about the women's role. This is a very interesting and satisfying answer to read. No examiner would deny it full marks!

3   Germany 1918–45

3.1   Was the Weimar Republic doomed from the start?

Topic Summary

As the First World War came to an end, Germany's Kaiser abdicated and a democratic government, the Weimar Republic, was set up. The new republic faced many problems. It got off to an unpopular start by agreeing to the Treaty of Versailles in 1919, which most Germans hated. Extremists tried to undermine the government and seize power. In 1923 the Ruhr was invaded by Belgium and France to force Germany to keep up reparations payments. The German economy collapsed under the impact of hyperinflation. In November 1923 the Nazis staged an unsuccessful putsch (rebellion) in Munich. However, the Republic recovered from these setbacks. Under the leadership of Stresemann, and with the help of US loans agreed in the Dawes Plan (1924), prosperity seemed to return, along with a golden era of art and culture. However, the Republic was less stable than it appeared, and many doubted that the good times could last.

What do I Need to Know?

You will need to understand how the end of the First World War affected German politics and society, and be able to explain why the Kaiser's regime collapsed and was replaced by the Weimar Republic. You should know why the Republic faced violent opposition from the start, and how the German people reacted to the terms of the Treaty of Versailles. You should be able to explain how and why the German economy collapsed in 1923, what the effects of this were, and how Stresemann overcame the crisis. You should be able to judge how far in the following years the republic was able to recover from the effects of the 1923 crisis, and to assess the achievements of the republic up to 1929.

Key Topics

How did Germany emerge from defeat in the First World War?

- By September 1918 the German armies on the Western Front were retreating. Defeat loomed. The German people were suffering severe food shortages because of the British naval blockade.

- In October 1918 the German navy in the port of Kiel mutinied when it was ordered to leave port and attack. By November, workers' councils, similar to soviets in Russia, were being formed all over the country. Germany was on the brink of revolution.
- Kaiser Wilhelm abdicated on 9 November 1918. Once he had gone, Germany hoped that the allies would agree a more lenient peace.
- Also on 9 November 1918, Ebert, leader of Germany's Social Democratic Party (SPD), declared that Germany was a republic. He became the first President.
- It was the new republican leaders who made peace with the Allies. This was a bad start. Many Germans did not believe that their armies had really been defeated. They called those who made peace the 'November Criminals'. Right-wing nationalists claimed that the politicians had betrayed Germany, and that she should have fought on. This was known as the 'stab-in-the-back' theory.
- The republic was also threatened by left-wing extremists who wanted Germany to become a communist state, like Russia. In January 1919 members of the communist Spartacus League – Spartacists – tried to stage a revolt in Berlin. The revolt failed, and its leaders, Karl Liebknecht and Rosa Luxemburg, were murdered. However, to crush the revolt the government had to rely on groups of ex-soldiers called Freikorps, who were bitter enemies of the communists.
- In January 1919 elections were held for a National Assembly. The Assembly met in Weimar to escape the violence in Berlin – hence the name 'Weimar Republic'.
- The Assembly agreed a constitution for the republic. Everyone over 21 could vote in elections for members of the Reichstag (Parliament). Election results were decided by proportional representation. Germany would have a chancellor (prime minister) as head of government, and a president (elected every seven years) as head of state.

Summary Box 1

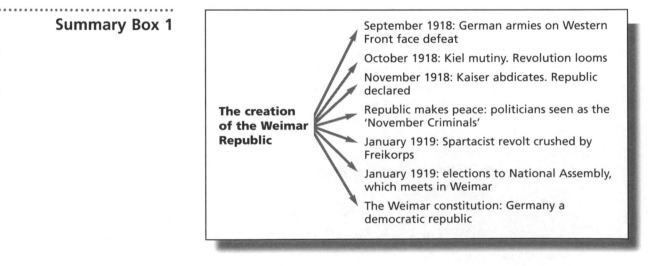

The creation of the Weimar Republic

September 1918: German armies on Western Front face defeat

October 1918: Kiel mutiny. Revolution looms

November 1918: Kaiser abdicates. Republic declared

Republic makes peace: politicians seen as the 'November Criminals'

January 1919: Spartacist revolt crushed by Freikorps

January 1919: elections to National Assembly, which meets in Weimar

The Weimar constitution: Germany a democratic republic

- The Weimar constitution had serious weaknesses. Proportional representation made it unlikely that any party would ever form a government on its own. All governments would then be coalitions, with a tendency to weakness. In addition, the constitution gave the president emergency powers to dissolve the Reichstag and rule by himself.

What was the impact of the Treaty of Versailles (1919) on the Republic?

- The Germans expected a treaty based on Wilson's Fourteen Points. They were furious at the harsh terms of the treaty.
- They called the treaty a 'diktat' (dictated peace). The Germans had no chance to negotiate – they were forced to accept it.
- By signing the treaty, the leaders of the Republic became even more unpopular. Extreme nationalists, who would never accept the treaty, now began to plan the overthrow of the Republic.
- In 1920 the government tried to disband the Freikorps. This provoked a rebellion. Units of Freikorps, under the leadership of Wolfgang Kapp, marched on Berlin. The army refused to intervene, and the government fled. But the Kapp putsch was defeated by a general strike of Berlin's workers, who hated the right-wing Freikorps and refused to co-operate with them.
- The government survived but the violence continued. During these years many prominent politicians were murdered by extremists.
- In 1921 the Allies fixed the amount of reparations Germany was to pay at £6600 million. The German economy, already weakened by the effects of war, was bound to struggle under this extra burden. At the end of 1922 the Germans said they could not pay. The French and Belgians invaded the Ruhr in January 1923 to seize coal and iron as reparations. The workers of the Ruhr went on strike. To support the strikers, the government printed money to pay them. This caused hyperinflation.
- In 1923 German money ceased to have any value. Businesses went bankrupt and people's savings were wiped out.
- Taking advantage of the crisis, in November 1923 Hitler attempted to seize power in Munich. This Munich putsch was a fiasco. Hitler was arrested and imprisoned, but was able to use his trial to gain publicity and make himself a national figure.
- In August 1923 Stresemann became chancellor. He knew that the Ruhr crisis would have to be settled. He agreed to resume paying reparations. By scrapping the worthless money and launching a new currency, the Rentenmark, he got the economy going again. In 1924 he agreed the Dawes Plan with the USA. This reduced Germany's annual reparations payments, and gave her US loans to build up the economy.

Summary Box 2

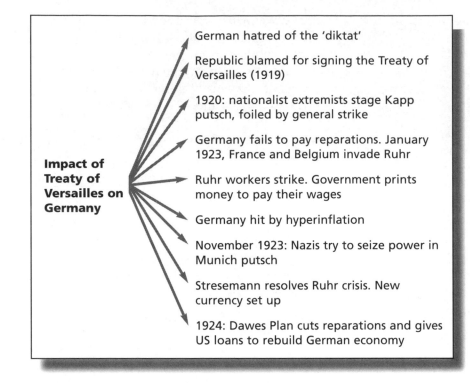

Impact of Treaty of Versailles on Germany

German hatred of the 'diktat'

Republic blamed for signing the Treaty of Versailles (1919)

1920: nationalist extremists stage Kapp putsch, foiled by general strike

Germany fails to pay reparations. January 1923, France and Belgium invade Ruhr

Ruhr workers strike. Government prints money to pay their wages

Germany hit by hyperinflation

November 1923: Nazis try to seize power in Munich putsch

Stresemann resolves Ruhr crisis. New currency set up

1924: Dawes Plan cuts reparations and gives US loans to rebuild German economy

To what extent did the Weimar Republic recover after 1923?

- Between 1924 and 1929 Germany received over 25 billion marks in loans. German industry was rebuilt.
- Chancellor Stresemann improved Germany's international position. The 1925 Locarno Pacts resolved Germany's borders with France and Belgium. In 1926 Germany was allowed to join the League of Nations.
- Stresemann believed in working with other countries to get the Treaty of Versailles revised, but many Germans criticised his moderate approach.
- The greater freedom that the Republic offered to artists and writers produced a cultural revival. German artists (such as George Grosz), architects, writers (like Brecht) and musicians became world famous. Berlin became the centre of this artistic revival.
- However, to a great extent, Germany's recovery after 1923 was an illusion. The economic recovery depended on loans, while some sectors of the economy, like agriculture, were in serious trouble.
- The political recovery also concealed the fact that many Germans hated the Republic, and would never accept the terms of the Versailles Treaty. The election of Hindenburg – a monarchist and one of Germany's war leaders – as president in 1925 was an indication of many Germans' true feelings.

What do I Know?

1. Name a German naval base at which there was a mutiny in October 1918.
2. Who was the first president of the Weimar Republic?
3. Which communist organisation staged a revolt against the republic in January 1919?
4. What name was given to the right-wing bands of ex-soldiers who were responsible for much of the violence in the early years of the Republic?
5. How did the Weimar Republic get its name?
6. What voting system was adopted by the Republic?
7. How long was the term of office of the president of the Republic?
8. What was the 'diktat'?
9. What was the sum agreed in 1921 that Germany would have to pay as reparations?
10. Which two countries invaded the Ruhr in 1923?
11. What was the reaction of the Ruhr workers to this invasion?
12. Which German politician solved the Ruhr crisis?
13. Name the new German currency set up in 1923.
14. Which international organisation was Germany permitted to join in 1926?
15. Name a famous German artist or writer of the Weimar period.

My score ...

What was the importance of:

- the 'stab-in-the back' theory
- the Kapp putsch
- hyperinflation
- the Dawes Plan?

Exam Type Question

The Optional Depth Studies are tested in Section C of Paper 1. On your chosen Depth Study you will have to answer **two** questions. The first will be a compulsory source-based question. There will be three sources and three sub-questions to answer. The second question will be structured, also consisting of three parts (worth 4, 6 and 10 marks for each part). There will be two of these structured questions, and you choose one.

Here is an example of a structured question on the Weimar Republic.

(a) Describe how a republic was formed in Germany at the end of the First World War. **(4 marks)**

(b) Explain why many Germans hated the Treaty of Versailles so much. **(6 marks)**

(c) Which of the following was the greatest threat to the Weimar Republic in 1923:
  (i) the invasion of the Ruhr;
  (ii) hyperinflation;
  (iii) the Munich putsch?
  Explain your answer. **(10 marks)**

Have a go yourself at parts (a) and (b) – here are a couple of students' answers to part (c).

Answer 1

I think the greatest threat to the Weimar Republic was the invasion of the Ruhr. This was obviously most important because foreign countries actually took over a part of Germany. The Ruhr was a vital part of Germany, being the most industrial part and most of Germany's wealth came from there. If Germany was going to pay reparations, the only way would be if the Ruhr was working. Once the French invaded, the Ruhr workers went on strike, so this meant that reparations would never be paid. Germany would go broke because it couldn't make any money from that area. The whole economy would collapse, which would be a disaster for everyone.

Answer 2

I think the greatest threat to Germany was the invasion of the Ruhr. The reason I think this is that the other two would not have happened without the invasion, so it has to be more important than them. The invasion was important in itself, because it deprived Germany of its most important industrial region, but it also sparked off a chain of events. Once the French marched in, the German government was forced to support the Ruhr workers who went on strike. The government couldn't just abandon the workers, so it paid their wages. Unfortunately the German government was already broke, so it had to print more money and this created hyperinflation. The hyperinflation was also a danger to the Republic, because of its effects on the German people. The economy was destroyed, people lost their businesses and their savings. This created a lot of discontent against the Republic, which in turn led to the third threat. Knowing how much hatred of the Republic there was and wanting to take advantage of the chaos, Hitler thought it would be a good time to try to take power. This was a threat to the Republic, though not serious as it turned out because the Munich putsch was a bit of a joke, but it showed that there were dangerous extremists around who were just waiting for a chance to attack the Republic. It's because all these events are linked that I think the one that started it all is the most important.

Examiner's Comments: Answer 1

5 out of 10

Although the question does not actually spell it out for you, you cannot produce a good answer without looking at all three of the given factors. The clue is in the word 'greatest'. If you look at just one factor, all you can discuss is whether or not it was a threat. You might decide it was a 'great' threat, but it's only by *comparing* it with other factors that you can decide it is the 'greatest'. This answer states that the invasion of the Ruhr was the most serious threat, but it ignores the other two factors. This won't earn a lot of credit, even though some perfectly good reasons are given for why the invasion was a great threat.

Answer 2

10 out of 10

Lots of answers fall short of the top level of marks, even though they discuss all the factors. They explain why each factor posed a threat, but their choice of 'greatest' is not based on a comparison of why one factor is more important *and* the others less important. The best way of establishing the relative importance of different factors is to show how they link together – answer 2 uses this technique very well. By demonstrating how one factor led to the next, it is a plausible argument to claim that the first is the *most* important. Another strength of the answer that each factor's *separate* importance is dealt with, as well as its interrelationship with the others.

3.2 Why was Hitler able to dominate Germany by 1934?

Topic Summary

In 1919 Hitler became one of the earliest members of the DAP, an extreme nationalist party which the following year became the NSDAP (Nazis). Hitler soon emerged as one of the Nazi Party leaders. The Nazis had many extreme ideas, but anti-Semitism (hatred of Jews) was one of the most important. During the 1920s the Nazis did not get much support. In 1923 Hitler tried to seize power in the Munich putsch, but he was arrested and imprisoned, and the Nazi Party was banned temporarily. His big chance came with the Great Depression which hit Germany at the end of 1929. Millions lost their jobs. The politicians of the Weimar Republic couldn't agree on what to do. In their desperation, people turned to extremists like the Nazis and communists. By 1932 support for the Nazis had grown so much that they had become the largest party in the Reichstag. In January 1933 President Hindenburg was persuaded to invite Hitler to become chancellor. New elections were announced. Hitler launched a terror campaign against his opponents. The elections gave Hitler the result he needed. With his allies he had enough votes to pass the Enabling Law in 1933, which gave him sweeping powers. Hitler was now dictator of Germany. The next year, in the Night of the Long Knives, Hitler turned on his opponents inside the Nazi Party. When Hindenburg died in August 1934, Hitler took over his powers. He was now Führer (leader) of Germany.

What do I Need to Know?

You will need to know about the early years of the Nazi Party, its ideas, and why initially it failed to win support. You should understand how the impact of the Depression benefited extremist parties in Germany, and how Hitler became chancellor at Hindenburg's invitation in January 1933. You must be able to explain how the Nazis won the election of March 1933, passed the Enabling Law, and established a dictatorship. You should understand the significance of the Night of the Long Knives in 1934, and know how Hitler was able to take total power after Hindenburg's death.

Key Topics

What did the Nazi Party stand for in the 1920s?

- In 1919 Hitler joined the DAP (German Workers' Party). This was an extreme nationalist party. His talent for public speaking ensured that he soon became one of its leaders.

- He was involved in writing DAP's 25-point programme. As well as many other ideas, DAP demanded the union of all Germans, living space for the German people, and profit sharing for workers in all large companies. At this early stage the party had some socialist ideas, but it got rid of these later. One thing it never changed was its anti-Semitism.
- In 1920 the party was renamed the NSDAP (National Socialist German Workers' Party, or 'Nazis'). The Nazis set up a paramilitary organisation known as the 'Stormtroopers' (the SA), and used the swastika as their party badge. The SA became notorious for their violence against the Nazis' opponents.
- The Nazis attracted support from many unemployed soldiers and others who were bitter about the outcome of the First World War. By 1923 Hitler thought he had enough support to seize power, but the Munich putsch was a failure. Hitler was arrested and put in prison until December 1924. He used his time in prison to write *Mein Kampf* ('My Struggle'). The Nazis were banned, and though the ban was lifted by 1925, for the rest of the 1920s they made only modest progress. Their annual Nuremberg national party rallies started in 1927. The apparent recovery of the Weimar Republic meant people had little time for extreme parties. In the 1928 election, the Nazis won only 12 Reichstag seats.

Summary Box 1

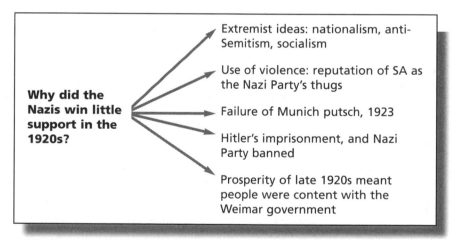

Why did the Nazis win little support in the 1920s?
- Extremist ideas: nationalism, anti-Semitism, socialism
- Use of violence: reputation of SA as the Nazi Party's thugs
- Failure of Munich putsch, 1923
- Hitler's imprisonment, and Nazi Party banned
- Prosperity of late 1920s meant people were content with the Weimar government

Why was Hitler able to become Chancellor by 1933?

- In October 1929, Stresemann died, and the Wall Street Crash in the US sparked off the Great Depression. US loans to Germany stopped and German industry collapsed. Millions were made unemployed. Desperate people turned to extremist parties for help. Support for the Nazis rapidly increased.
- The Weimar politicians could not cope with the effects of the Depression. No one party had enough support in the Reichstag to form a strong government. From 1930 President Hindenburg ruled by decree, and appointed his own chancellors. Between 1930 and 1932 Heinrich Brüning of the Centre Party was chancellor.

- As a result of the July 1932 elections the Nazis became the largest party in the Reichstag with 230 seats. Although this fell to 196 seats in the November 1932 elections, the Nazis still had more seats than any other party. However, this was still nowhere near enough seats to form a government on their own.

- Hindenburg was surrounded by a small group of conservative advisers who plotted against each other for power. One of them, von Papen, thought he could use Hitler to make himself more powerful. He persuaded Hindenburg to invite Hitler to become chancellor, but of a coalition government with only three Nazis in it. Von Papen would be vice-chancellor.

- Hindenburg reluctantly agreed, and on 30 January 1933 Hitler became chancellor.

- New elections were called for in March 1933. The election campaign gave Hitler ample opportunity to win full control. He banned the Communist Party and shut down their newspapers. He used the SA to intimidate political opponents. On 27 February 1933 the Reichstag building was destroyed by fire. A communist, van der Lubbe, was found inside the burning building and was blamed for the fire. Hitler used the fire to intensify anti-communist hysteria. Hindenburg passed an emergency decree allowing Hitler to arrest communist leaders, and ban his opponents from holding political meetings.

- The election results were good for Hitler. The Nazis won 288 seats out of 647. By banning the 81 communist deputies, and by promising the Centre Party not to harm the Catholic Church, Hitler with his allies had enough votes to pass the Enabling Law, which gave him power to make laws without referring to the Reichstag.

- The Enabling Law of March 1933 made Hitler dictator over Germany. In July he banned all other political parties.

- The only significant threats to Hitler now came from within the Nazi Party. The SA had become a major problem. Röhm, leader of the SA, had left-wing views which would offend the businessmen that Hitler now wanted to work with. Röhm also wanted to merge the SA into the German army, but Hitler feared this would lose him the army's support.

- On 30 June 1934 Hitler ordered his elite bodyguard (the SS) to arrest and murder the leaders of the SA. Hundreds of SA members and others of Hitler's opponents such as Schleicher, the ex-chancellor, were killed. Hitler pretended that Röhm was planning a revolution to justify his actions. In reality, Röhm's 'crime' was to be a potential rival to Hitler.

- On 2 August 1934 Hindenburg died. His death allowed Hitler to declare himself Führer (leader) of Germany. The army was made to swear an oath of loyalty to Hitler. Hitler had achieved total power.

Summary Box 2

Impact of the Great Depression: millions unemployed, extremist parties gain support

Weimar democracy collapses, Hindenburg rules by decree

Nazis become largest party in Reichstag, 1932

Hitler's steps to power, 1929–34

Von Papen persuades Hindenburg to make Hitler chancellor, January 1933

Hitler uses election campaign and Reichstag fire to crush communists

March 1933 elections: Hitler wins enough seats to pass Enabling Law. Germany becomes a dictatorship

June 1934, Night of the Long Knives: Hitler moves against SA, and has opponents murdered

August 1934: Hindenburg's death. Hitler becomes Führer

What do I Know?

1   How many points were there in the 1920 programme of the German Workers' Party?
2   What new name did the German Workers' Party adopt in 1920?
3   Give another name for the 'Stormtroopers'.
4   Name the book that Hitler wrote whilst in prison.
5   From 1927, where did the Nazis hold their national party rallies?
6   Which prominent German politician died in October 1929?
7   Who was chancellor between 1930 and 1932?
8   Who persuaded Hindenburg to appoint Hitler as chancellor?
9   How many Nazis were in Hitler's first Cabinet?
10   Who was blamed for the Reichstag Fire?
11   Which law passed in March 1933 gave Hitler the power of a dictator?
12   Which party supported this law when Hitler promised not to harm the Catholic Church?
13   Who was leader of the SA?
14   Which former chancellor was murdered in the Night of the Long Knives?
15   Whose death in August 1934 enabled Hitler to take the title of Führer?

My score …

What was the importance of:
- the SA
- the Reichstag fire
- the Enabling Law
- the Night of the Long Knives?

Exam Type Question

The Optional Depth Studies are tested in Section C of Paper 1. On your chosen Depth Study you will have to answer two questions. The first will be a compulsory source-based question. There will be three sources and three sub-questions to answer. The second question will be structured, also consisting of three parts (worth 4, 6 and 10 marks for each part). There will be two of these structured questions, and you choose one.

Here is an example of a structured question on Hitler's rise to power.

(a) Describe the main ideas that the Nazi Party stood for in the 1920s. **(4 marks)**

(b) Explain why the Nazi Party attracted little support during the 1920s. **(6 marks)**

(c) Explain how the following together contributed to Hitler becoming chancellor in January 1933:
   (i)   the impact of the Great Depression;
   (ii) increasing Nazi support in elections, 1930–2;
   (iii) political intrigues involving Hindenburg. **(10 marks)**

Have a go yourself at parts (a) and (c) – here are a couple of students' answers to part (b).

Answer 1

There were reasons why the Nazis did not win much support at that time. They were extremists and they were violent. People thought the Weimar Republic was doing alright. Hitler was in prison some of the time, so this meant that the Nazi Party was without its leader and it lost direction without him.

Answer 2

The best explanation of why the Nazis did not get too much support in the 1920s is that the Weimar Republic was doing pretty well and most Germans were prospering, so they weren't interested in a party that had an extreme and violent image. It was a different matter after the Wall Street Crash. When things started to go wrong, people got fed up with the Weimar government and supported the extremists who said they could do something about the Depression. In the 1920s you had to be one of society's losers to support the Nazis. They attracted support from those who never really got over Germany's defeat in the war – a lot of cranks and anti-Semites. Because of this, they weren't regarded as respectable. No decent person would think of joining them.

Examiner's Comments: Answer 1

4 out of 6

In part (b) questions you will invariably be asked to provide *reasons* for something. However, you are also asked to *explain* the reasons. Just giving a reason doesn't count as an explanation. This answer illustrates the point well. It starts by identifying three reasons – the Nazis were extreme, they were violent, and the Weimar Republic was doing well. But it's only when it gets to the fourth reason – Hitler's imprisonment – that any explanation occurs. As there are four reasons here, and one is explained, four marks are appropriate.

Answer 2

6 out of 6

The superior quality of an answer that moves straight into *explaining* reasons is immediately obvious. By comparing the impact the Nazis were able to have *after* the Wall Street Crash with the situation in the 1920s, the writer successfully explains why Weimar's earlier prosperity prevented the Nazis gaining support. The answer goes on to establish a further reason, which is that the Nazis had no hope of achieving respectability in the 1920s because of their extremism which was bound only to appeal to a narrow section of society. Two reasons clearly explained like this would earn all available marks.

3.3 How effectively did the Nazis control Germany, 1933–45?

Topic Summary

The Nazis used different ways to try to control the German people. Goebbels, the Minister of Propaganda, made sure that the Nazis' message was constantly in the public eye: the mass media were under Nazi Party control; the Nazi flag was displayed everywhere; there were mass rallies and demonstrations of support; even films and literature had to be approved by the Nazis. This made sure that the German people never heard any opposing views. The other approach used by the Nazis was terror. The secret police, the Gestapo, hunted down anyone suspected of being an opponent. Concentration camps were set up where 'undesirables' could be locked away. The courts were taken over to make sure that the 'right' verdict was always reached when opponents were put on trial. At first even the Catholic Church was prepared to work with the Nazis, though it later changed its mind. Despite all these controls, there was still some opposition. Many churchmen spoke out against the brutality of the Nazi regime, many senior army officers and members of the upper classes were never won over to Nazism, and youth groups resisted the restrictions that the Nazis tried to impose on young people. However, because of the nature of the Nazi regime, it is impossible to know how much opposition there really was.

What do I Need to Know?

You will need to understand how the Nazis controlled the German people through a mixture of propaganda and repression. You should know how the Nazis made use of culture and the mass media to ensure that people were indoctrinated with Nazi beliefs. You should also be aware that these methods did not always work, and that there was some opposition to the Nazis. You should know about these opposition groups, and why they opposed the Nazis.

Key Topics

How did the Nazis use culture and the mass media to control people?

- Goebbels was in charge of the Ministry for People's Enlightenment and Propaganda.
- This ministry controlled the mass media: radio, press and films all had their output controlled.

- All areas of culture were also Nazified: literature, art, theatre. It became impossible for non-Nazi views to be heard. Public book burnings occurred, when books by Jewish or communist authors were destroyed.
- Radios were made available cheaply so that the Nazi message could be sent into every home.
- Nazi flags and posters were everywhere. The Nazis organised huge rallies, like the annual gathering in Nuremberg.
- The greatest propaganda opportunity was the 1936 Berlin Olympics. Foreign visitors were impressed by the efficiency of the organisation of the Games, and the brutality of the Nazi state was kept out of sight. The Germans won the most medals, but Hitler's triumph was undermined by the achievements of Jesse Owens, a black American athlete – as far as the Nazis were concerned, Owens was a member of an inferior race.

How effectively did the Nazis deal with their political opponents?

- The Enabling Law of 1933 gave Hitler the power to crush his political opponents. All other political parties were banned. Many socialists and communists fled the country.
- The SS under Heinrich Himmler was Hitler's main security force. They ran the concentration camps and the secret police. The Gestapo hunted down anyone suspected of disloyalty to the regime. Networks of informers made it unsafe for anyone to express anti-Nazi views.
- Enemies of the Nazis were sent to concentration camps where conditions were brutal. SS Death's Head units were in charge of these camps.
- The courts were taken over by the Nazis. Judges had to be loyal to the Nazi Party.
- By 1939, over 150,000 people were being held as political prisoners in Nazi Germany.

How much opposition was there to the Nazi regime?

- Because of the secretive nature of the Nazi state, it is hard to know how much opposition there was. Many opponents left the country.
- At first, the Catholic Church agreed not to interfere in German politics in return for a promise that the Nazis would not interfere in religion. This agreement was called the Concordat (1933). However, Hitler didn't keep the bargain. By 1937 the Concordat broke down, and Pope Pius XI denounced the Nazis as anti-Christian. Many churchmen of all religions opposed the Nazis. Some like Pastor Niemoller were sent to labour camps; some were murdered.
- Many young people rejected the influence of the Hitler Youth. Members of the 'Swing' movement were condemned by the Nazis because of their interest in American and British popular

music. Groups of teenagers such as the Navajos Gang and the Edelweiss Pirates were generally regarded by the Nazis as no more than delinquents. However, during the war they got involved in spreading anti-Nazi propaganda and, in 1944, took part in an attack in which a Gestapo officer was killed. After this, some were arrested and publicly executed.

- Hans and Sophie Scholl led a student group in Munich called the White Rose Movement. They were executed in 1943 for anti-Nazi activities.

- Some of the most dangerous opposition to the regime came from members of the upper classes and army. Once the war started they feared that Hitler would lead Germany to disaster. In 1944 a group of army officers attempted to assassinate Hitler, but this 'July Bomb Plot' failed and the plotters were rounded up and executed. Rommel, one of Germany's greatest generals, committed suicide before he could be arrested.

What do I Know?

1 Who was the Nazis' Minister of Propaganda?
2 What did the Nazis do with books written by Jewish and communist authors?
3 Where were the Olympic Games held in 1936?
4 Who was the outstanding athlete of the 1936 Olympics?
5 What agreement was signed in 1933 between the Nazis and the Roman Catholic Church?
6 Which Pope denounced the Nazis in 1937 as anti-Christian?
7 Name a German churchman who spoke out against the Nazis.
8 Name the youth movement whose members were condemned as degenerate by the Nazis because they were interested in US and British popular culture.
9 Which youth group took part in an attack on the Gestapo in 1944?
10 Which student opposition group was led by Hans and Sophie Scholl?
11 Who attempted to assassinate Hitler in July 1944?
12 Which famous German general committed suicide because of his suspected involvement in this assassination attempt?
13 Who was leader of the SS?
14 Which section of the SS ran the concentration camps?
15 What was the job of the Gestapo?

My score …

What was the importance of:

- the Nuremberg rallies
- the 1936 Olympic Games
- the Concordat
- concentration camps?

Exam Type Question

The Optional Depth Studies are tested in Section C of Paper 1. On your chosen Depth Study you will have to answer **two** questions. The first will be a compulsory source-based question. There will be three sources and three sub-questions to answer. The source-based question carries 20 marks in total, with the three parts each being worth 6, 7 and 7 marks, though not necessarily in that order.

Although the questions are source-based and test source-handling skills, they also require you to use your knowledge.

The second question will be structured, also consisting of three parts (worth 4, 6 and 10 marks for each part). There will be two of these structured questions, and you choose one.

Take a look at the following source-based example. Study the sources carefully, and then answer the questions which follow.

Source A

▲ A 1933 cartoon showing the SA burning books by Jewish and communist authors.

Source B

Attention! The Führer is speaking on the radio. On Wednesday 21 March the Führer is speaking from 11.00 to 11.50 a.m. The district Party headquarters has ordered that all factory owners, department stores, offices, shops, pubs, and blocks of flats put up loudspeakers an hour before the broadcast so that the whole workforce and all national comrades can participate.

▲ An announcement in a local newspaper, March 1934.

Source C

◄ A poster of Hitler from the 1930s.

> **(a)** Study Source A.
> Do you think this cartoon was published by the Nazis or by their opponents? Use the source and your knowledge to explain your answer. **(6 marks)**
>
> **(b)** Study Source B.
> Why do you think this announcement was put into the newspaper? Use the source and your own knowledge to explain your answer. **(7 marks)**
>
> **(c)** Study Source C.
> Do you think this poster would help the Nazis maintain control over Germany? Use the source and your knowledge to explain your answer. **(7 marks)**

Have a go yourself at parts (a) and (c) – here are a couple of students' answers to part (b).

Answer 1

I think this was put into the newspaper to make sure that everyone would hear the Führer speaking. If people read the newspaper they would know that they must put up loudspeakers everywhere. Then at the right time everyone would be able to listen, no matter where they were. It was obviously very important for everyone to know what Hitler had to say, so the newspaper made sure they all knew what to do.

Answer 2

The Nazis made constant use of the radio to transmit their propaganda messages to the German people. They regarded propaganda as one of the most important ways in which to control the population. Obviously by putting this notice in the local paper, the Nazis would make sure that everyone heard what Hitler had to say. Even more important, people wouldn't dare not to put up loudspeakers because this would identify them as an opponent. The Nazis wanted to make sure they got their message into every aspect of German life. It wasn't enough to put the speech on the radio, they had to make sure that people listened, no matter where they were, at home, at work, at the shops, or in the pub.

Examiner's Comments: Answer 1

3 out of 7

The question asks you to use the source *and* your own knowledge. Although this answer is sensible and the student obviously understands what was going on, there's no evidence in the answer of any knowledge that doesn't come straight from the source itself. Because the answer is limited in this way, it can't earn more than half marks.

Answer 2

7 out of 7

This answer provides a good contrast to the first example, because the writer provides contextual knowledge right away. Nowhere in the source does it tell you that the Nazis commonly used radio propaganda or that they placed great importance on propaganda, so this obviously comes from the writer's own knowledge. The answer introduces those ideas to help explain why the local Nazi Party put this notice into the paper, just as the question requires. It also uses the source, and illustrates how the issue of propaganda was all about social control. It's quite a short answer, but perfectly sufficient.

3.4 What was it like to live in Nazi Germany?

Topic Summary

The Nazis put great priority on winning over the hearts and minds of the young. They set up youth movements for children and young people in different age groups, and they tightly controlled education. They had traditional views about women in society. They thought the job of women was to stay at home and have children. There were few good employment opportunities for women. However, the Nazis knew that solving the unemployment crisis was one of their most important tasks. Re-armament produced many new jobs in industry and the armed forces. Public works schemes further cut the number of unemployed. On the face of it, the Nazis dealt successfully with unemployment, but German workers paid a price. Free trade unions were banned, wages remained low, and consumer goods were in short supply. There were also many groups, and notably the Jews, who became targets of Nazi persecution. From 1933, persecution of the Jews became progressively worse, and large numbers emigrated to avoid it. In 1938 Jewish shops and synagogues were attacked in *Kristallnacht*. Other minorities also suffered. Anyone who did not conform to the Nazis' ideas of racial perfection was at risk: homosexuals, the mentally disabled, tramps and beggars, and people labelled as 'gypsies'. This persecution reached its peak during the war when the Nazis launched the 'Final Solution' – the mass murder of Jews in the death camps. The war brought first triumph and then disaster to Germany. As the tide of war turned against Germany, civilians suffered greatly. Food was in short supply, and Allied bombing reduced many German cities to rubble.

What do I Need to Know?

You will need to understand why the Nazis placed so much importance on indoctrinating the young, and how they went about achieving this in education and by setting up youth movements. You should know how women were treated in Nazi Germany. You should be able to explain how the Nazis managed the economy, and the impact this had on the workforce. You should be aware of the Nazi persecution of minority groups, and how this developed into the 'Final Solution'. You should know how the Second World War affected life in Germany.

Key Topics

How did young people react to the Nazi regime?

- The Hitler Youth was founded in 1926. It already had 100,000 members when the Nazis took power.
- There were different branches of the Hitler Youth movement for girls and boys, and for age groups. Only boys between 14 and 18 were full members of the Hitler Youth; girls between 14 and 17 were members of the League of German Maidens. Children were indoctrinated with Nazi ideas, and prepared for their roles in life – boys as soldiers, girls as mothers.
- Originally membership was optional, but the Hitler Youth Law of 1936 made it compulsory. Many young people were happy to join. There weren't many other organisations for them, and many enjoyed the kinds of activities – sports, camping, marching and so on – that the Hitler Youth encouraged.
- The Nazis controlled education. They dictated the subjects that were to be taught and made sure that Nazi ideas and racial beliefs were included in the teaching of subjects like History and Biology. Teachers were forced to join the Nazi teachers' organisation.

How successful were Nazi policies towards women and the family?

- Motherhood and family life were an important part of Nazi propaganda. The Nazis had traditional and conservative views about family matters, and the roles of men and women.
- Women were not equal with men in Nazi Germany. They were expected to remain at home and raise children. If they did work, the better jobs were closed to them.
- Hitler was alarmed at the falling birth rate and women were encouraged to have large families. The Mother's Cross was given to women with more than three children, with the golden version of the cross awarded for eight or more.

Did most people in Germany benefit from Nazi rule?

- When Hitler came to power 6 million were unemployed. He promised to deal with unemployment.
- Re-armament created many jobs. Armaments industries employed more workers, and the introduction of conscription meant that numbers in the armed forces increased rapidly.
- Public works schemes, such as the construction of autobahns (motorways), also made more jobs.
- By 1938, there was almost no unemployment in Germany.
- However, there was a price to be paid. Workers had no rights, they had to join the Nazi Labour Front, and free trade unions were banned. Wages stayed low while working hours increased. There were few consumer goods to purchase.

Summary Box 1

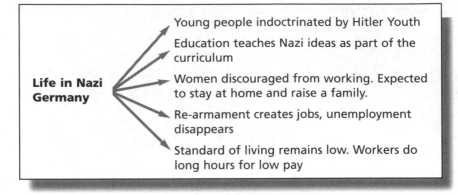

Life in Nazi Germany

- Young people indoctrinated by Hitler Youth
- Education teaches Nazi ideas as part of the curriculum
- Women discouraged from working. Expected to stay at home and raise a family.
- Re-armament creates jobs, unemployment disappears
- Standard of living remains low. Workers do long hours for low pay

Why did the Nazis persecute many groups in German society?

- Nazis believed that the Germans were the master race. Their racial group, the Aryans, were supposed to be tall and blond with blue eyes. They believed that other races were inferior (or *Untermenschen*), and they reserved a particular hatred for the Jews.

- Nazi propaganda blamed the Jews for everything that had gone wrong in Germany, including defeat in the First World War. Once in power, Hitler began to persecute them.

- From 1933 Jews were banned from the professions and were not allowed to work for the government. The SA organised boycotts of Jewish shops and intimidated anyone who dared to shop in them.

- In 1935 the Nuremberg Laws deprived Jews of citizenship and forbade marriages between Jews and non-Jews. Many Jews fled the country.

- In 1938 a German diplomat was shot dead in Paris by a Jewish assassin. As a reprisal, the Nazis organised *Kristallnacht* (the Night of Broken Glass) in which Nazi mobs attacked and burnt Jewish shops, homes, businesses and synagogues. Over a hundred Jews were murdered in the violence of *Kristallnacht*.

- The Nazis persecuted many other groups who were thought inferior. Many homosexuals were sent to concentration camps. Mentally disabled people were compulsorily sterilised. Later, many disabled people were murdered in a euthanasia programme. Even beggars were rounded up and imprisoned in the labour camps.

- During the war, when Germany captured huge areas of eastern Europe, millions of Jews came under Nazi control. In January 1942, at the Wannsee Conference, it was decided to exterminate them. The Nazis called this the 'Final Solution' to their 'Jewish problem'.

- By the summer of 1942 the extermination camps had started the process which led to the murder of 6 million Jews over the next three years.

- Jews from all over Europe were transported by rail to the death camps. Most were killed in gas chambers soon after their arrival. A smaller number were temporarily reprieved to work in appalling conditions in the camps. Their possessions were looted by the Nazis, who even removed gold teeth from corpses. The slaughter of the Jews in the death camps is known as the Holocaust.

- After the war, trials of Nazi war criminals were held at Nuremberg. Some, like Himmler and Goering, committed suicide; others were executed.

Summary Box 2

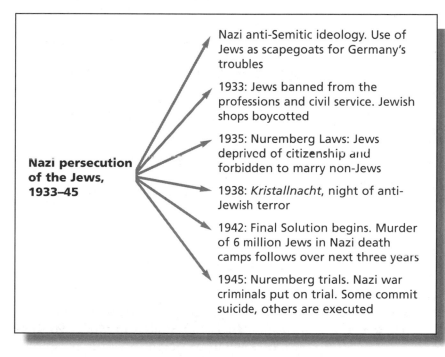

Nazi persecution of the Jews, 1933–45

Nazi anti-Semitic ideology. Use of Jews as scapegoats for Germany's troubles

1933: Jews banned from the professions and civil service. Jewish shops boycotted

1935: Nuremberg Laws: Jews deprived of citizenship and forbidden to marry non-Jews

1938: *Kristallnacht*, night of anti-Jewish terror

1942: Final Solution begins. Murder of 6 million Jews in Nazi death camps follows over next three years

1945: Nuremberg trials. Nazi war criminals put on trial. Some commit suicide, others are executed

How did the coming of war change life in Nazi Germany?

- The start of the war saw great German victories. Victory was won quickly and easily so there was little impact on life in Germany itself.

- After the attack on the Soviet Union in 1941, the war began to affect Germany more. Supplies were needed for the army, and shortages became more obvious at home. In 1942 Albert Speer was made armaments minister and prepared the country for 'total war'. Factories worked longer hours. Food rations were cut.

- From 1942 Allied bombing raids began to hit German cities. Civilian casualties mounted. As the war went on, these raids intensified, reducing large areas of many cities to rubble. In one raid on Dresden in February 1945, 135,000 civilians died.

- By the end of the war, the civilian population of Germany had suffered great hardship. There were more than 3 million civilians dead, much of the surviving population was starving, and their country had been reduced to ruins.

What do I Know?

1. In which year was the Hitler Youth formed?
2. Which branch of the Hitler Youth was for girls of between 14 and 17 years of age?
3. What was the purpose of the Hitler Youth Law of 1936?
4. Why were the Nazis so keen to have their version of Biology taught in schools?
5. To how many children did a woman have to give birth to win the golden Mother's Cross?
6. Approximately how many Germans were unemployed when Hitler took power?
7. One way the Nazis made jobs was to build autobahns. What were these?
8. Name the Nazi trade union organisation that all workers had to join.
9. What did the Nazis call the ideal Germanic racial group?
10. What word did the Nazis have for all races they regarded as inferior human beings?
11. From what jobs were Jews banned in 1933?
12. What was the German name for the 'Night of Broken Glass'?
13. Name a group other than the Jews who were persecuted by the Nazis.
14. Who was put in charge of organising the German economy for 'total war' in 1942?
15. Where were the trials of Nazi war criminals held in 1945?

My score …

What was the importance of:
- the Hitler Youth
- the Nuremberg Laws
- *Kristallnacht*
- the Wannsee Conference?

Exam Type Question

The Optional Depth Studies are tested in Section C of Paper 1. On your chosen Depth Study you will have to answer two questions. The first will be a compulsory source-based question. There will be three sources, and three sub-questions to answer. The second will be a structured question consisting of three parts (4/6/10 marks). There will be two questions, and you choose one.

Here is an example of a structured question on life in Nazi Germany.

(a) What did the Nazis believe about the differences between racial groups? **(4 marks)**

(b) Why did the Nazis attack Jews and Jewish property on *Kristallnacht*? **(6 marks)**

(c) 'The only reason the Nazis started the Holocaust in 1942 was their hatred of Jews.' Do you agree with this statement? Explain your answer. **(10 marks)**

Have a go yourself at parts (a) and (b), but here are a couple of students' answers to part (c).

Answer 1

It isn't true that the only reason why the Nazis launched the Final Solution in 1942 was their hatred of Jews. That was obviously one reason, because they wouldn't have wanted to exterminate them otherwise. Anti-Semitism was one of the Nazis most important ideas. Hitler had hated the Jews from the start and he blamed them for Germany losing the First World War. But there were other reasons why they started the Holocaust in 1942. For example they had conquered countries like Poland that had large Jewish populations and by 1942 they were invading the Soviet Union, so there were lots of new areas where the Nazis were in charge and they had Jewish populations, so that's another reason why it happened in 1942.

Answer 2

There's a difference in explaining why the Nazis started the Holocaust, and why they started it in 1942. In a way, the only reason for the Holocaust was the Nazis' hatred of the Jews. Hitler believed the Jews were inferior beings and he blamed them for everything that had gone wrong in Germany. He was prepared to do them harm. The Holocaust could not have happened without this deep and irrational hatred. However, this is no explanation for why it happened when it did. The Nazis did not start the Holocaust in 1933, when they came to power. Certainly they persecuted the Jews, but they didn't start an extermination campaign. By 1942, though, things had changed. The Nazis had captured much of eastern Europe. In these countries were large Jewish populations, so the Nazis simply had more Jews to deal with than ever before. The other, crucial factor was that it was now war-time. The Nazis could now hide their murder much more effectively than ever they could in peace-time. Their death squads had already been active during the invasion of the Soviet Union. In other words, the Nazis felt they had a 'Jewish Problem' to solve, and there were no restraints on how they solved it. So you can't say that anti-Semitism was the only reason for the Holocaust, because that doesn't explain why it occurred exactly how and when it did.

Examiner's Comments: Answer 1

7 out of 10

Questions that give you a causal factor (a reason) and ask whether it was the *only* reason should always be met with the response, 'Of course not!' There's always more than one reason. The writer of this answer clearly knows that you must not fall into the trap of writing only about the given factor, so another reason is included and explained. This is fine, particularly as the answer also explains the given factor. So here we have an answer that understands that events have multiple causes. What it lacks is any explanation of how those causes might relate to each other, or the different part that each might play in an explanation. Nonetheless, answers based on multiple causes can earn a good share of the marks. This has only the two causes and is rather limited, but it would still possibly earn seven marks.

Answer 2

10 out of 10

This answer, too, accepts that there must be multiple causes, but it also understands that these causes are not all the same in nature. There are causes which explain why an event occurs at a specific time. These are often known as short-term causes, or 'triggers'. In this answer, the triggers for the Holocaust were the German conquests of eastern Europe, particularly during 1941–2. But these conquests do not, of course, explain why the Nazis hated the Jews, and without this hatred there would have been no Holocaust. The hatred, then, is a long-term cause, or 'precondition'. A proper explanation of why an event occurred will always deal with these different types of causes, and will also earn the highest marks. This answer is worth ten out of ten.

4 Russia 1905–41

4.1 Why did the Tsarist regime collapse in 1917?

Topic Summary

Before the First World War Russia was the most backward of the great powers. Its ruler was Tsar Nicholas II. He ruled as an autocrat – all power was in his hands. Although well meaning, he was a weak ruler, unable to deal with the great problems Russia faced. Most Russians were poor peasants, barely scraping a living from the land. Industries were beginning to develop, and social conditions in the growing cities were very bad. The Russian people wanted more freedom, but the Tsar refused to give it. In 1905, after Russia's disastrous defeat in the Russo-Japanese War, a revolution took place. The Tsar survived the revolution only by promising to allow a parliament (Duma) to meet. The Tsar's position was threatened again by the outbreak of the First World War. Russia's armies were poorly-led and badly-supplied. As the war dragged on with no victory in sight, disillusionment with the Tsar grew. There was also public concern over the influence a Siberian peasant, Rasputin, had over the Tsar and Tsarina. Finally, a wave of strikes in March 1917 in the capital, Petrograd, sparked off another revolution. This time, the Tsar's power collapsed. He abdicated, and a Provisional Government was set up to run the country until a new government could be elected.

What do I Need to Know?

You will need to know about the main features of Russian life before the First World War – the different social classes, how the country was governed, what changes were occurring – and be able to explain why revolution broke out in 1905. You should assess the impact of the 1905 revolution and be able to judge the extent to which the Tsarist regime had recovered by the outbreak of war in 1914. You will need to know why the First World War was so disastrous for Russia, and explain how and why the Tsar was overthrown in the revolution of March 1917.

Key Topics

How well did the Tsarist regime deal with the problems of ruling Russia up to 1914?

- Before the First World War, Russia was ruled by a Tsar (the word means 'emperor'). He had total power. Russia had no parliament or elections. The Tsar's power was supported by the Russian Orthodox Church, and by the wealthy landowning class.

- The Tsar from 1894 was Nicholas II. He was sincere and hard working, but he was also weak and indecisive.
- Russia was huge. The problems of ruling a vast empire were great, particularly as Russia was so backward.
- Russia was still a rural society. Most Russians were poor peasants. Until 1861, when they were finally freed, most had been serfs (peasant slaves) and their lives had been totally controlled by the landowners. The peasants needed more land, but most of the land remained in the hands of rich landowners. The more liberal landowners began to press the Tsar for reforms through the local councils, known as *zemstvos*. Agriculture needed to be modernised: famines were common, as were peasant uprisings against the landowners.
- Encouraged by Witte, the Minister of Finance from 1892, industry was developing. However, living and working conditions in the new industrial cities were poor, so the cities were breeding grounds of discontent and revolutionary ideas.
- Russia had a long revolutionary tradition. Most revolutionaries were from the middle classes, who were denied any political rights. Many revolutionary groups plotted to overthrow the Tsar. The Tsar's secret police, the Okhrana, constantly repressed these groups, and most revolutionaries spent some time in prison or in exile.
- The most important of the revolutionary groups were the Marxists. In 1903 their party, the Social Democratic Party, split into two groups: the Bolsheviks ('majority') and the Mensheviks ('minority'). The Bolsheviks were led by Lenin.

Summary Box 1

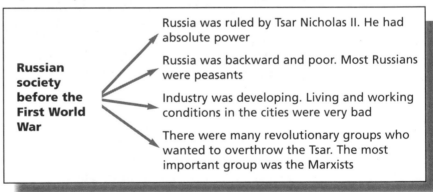

Russian society before the First World War

Russia was ruled by Tsar Nicholas II. He had absolute power

Russia was backward and poor. Most Russians were peasants

Industry was developing. Living and working conditions in the cities were very bad

There were many revolutionary groups who wanted to overthrow the Tsar. The most important group was the Marxists

How did the Tsar survive the 1905 revolution?

- In 1904 war broke out between Russia and Japan. The Russians expected to win. Instead they suffered disastrous defeat. The decisive battle was naval, at Tsushima in May 1905. Russia was forced to make peace.
- The humiliation of defeat helped spark off the 1905 revolution in Russia. The middle classes demanded political reforms, and strikes broke out, with workers demanding better conditions and pay.
- On 9 January 1905 a mass demonstration in St Petersburg, led by Father Gapon, planned to march to the Tsar's Winter Palace. The crowd was attacked by troops and around 200 people were

killed. The public outrage at the events of 'Bloody Sunday' plunged Russia into full-scale revolt. Across the country, the authorities lost control. Mutinies occurred in the armed forces, most famously on the battleship *Potemkin*.

- Soviets – workers' councils – were set up all over the country. These councils took over factories and much of the work of local government. The St Petersburg Soviet was almost an alternative national government.

- By October 1905 even the Tsar realised that he would have to make concessions. He issued his October Manifesto, promising that elections would be held and a parliament (Duma) established. This was what the middle classes wanted. Like the Tsar, they had become alarmed by the growing power and influence of revolutionaries in the soviets, and now wanted the revolution to come to an end. By splitting his opponents, the Tsar was able to regain control. Many of the soviets' leaders were arrested, and an attempted uprising in Moscow in December was repressed.

- The Tsar had made concessions in bad faith. He had no intention of keeping his promises unless he had to. When the first Duma met in 1906 and demanded land reforms, the Tsar dissolved it. A second Duma in 1907 met the same fate. The third Duma survived, but only because the Tsar changed the voting rules and so ensured that the Duma was composed mainly of his supporters.

- The Tsar's Prime Minister until 1911, Peter Stolypin, fiercely repressed any remaining signs of revolution.

- However, Russia was changed by the 1905 revolution. The fact that a Duma existed at all meant that some free political activity was now possible. The Tsar no longer had total power. Even Stolypin realised that further reforms were necessary. He made it possible for peasants to borrow money to buy land and create their own farms, instead of relying on the old communal form of agriculture. However, most peasants were reluctant to change, and progress in modernising agriculture was slow.

Summary Box 2

The 1905 revolution and its results

- 1904: the Russo-Japanese War breaks out. Russia defeated by 1905

- Outbreak of unrest in Russia: events of Bloody Sunday, January 1905, spark off revolution

- Nationwide unrest, mutinies, strikes, peasant uprisings, setting up of soviets

- October Manifesto. Tsar promises elections and Duma

- Concessions win over middle classes. Soviets crushed, Moscow rising repressed (December 1905)

- Tsar dissolves First and Second Duma. Third Duma acceptable to him, 1907

- Stolypin's repression and reforms

How far was the Tsar weakened by the First World War?

- Germany declared war on Russia on 1 August 1914. After Russia's early advance into East Prussia was halted in the autumn of 1914 at Tannenberg, fighting on the Eastern Front became bogged down, with neither side able to win a decisive victory.

- Russia's armies were badly-led and poorly-supplied. After early defeats, the Tsar had taken over personal command of the armies. In reality he was just a figurehead, but his involvement took him away from Petrograd (the name of the capital had been changed from the German-sounding St Petersburg at the start of the war) and left the government in the hands of his wife.

- Although Russia's armies were manned by peasants, their absence from the fields made little difference to agriculture. Throughout the war Russia produced plenty of food. The problem was that transport was so poor that not enough food got to the armies, or to the cities. From the start of the war, there were food shortages.

- The Russian economy could not cope with the demands of war. The government printed money to pay for the war, causing inflation, and wages did not keep up with higher prices. Many workers lost their jobs when factories closed as consumers no longer had money to spend.

- The Duma leaders were frustrated at the Tsar's refusal to appoint a representative government that would unite the people in the war effort.

- Concern grew at the influence Rasputin had over the Tsarina. With the Tsar away, the Tsarina relied almost entirely on Rasputin's advice. Ministers were appointed or sacked according to his whim. Finally, in December 1916, a group of noblemen murdered him.

Why was the revolution of March 1917 successful?

- By March 1917, the Tsar had lost the support of almost all groups in the country.

- Trouble broke out in the capital, Petrograd. A wave of strikes in March proved impossible for the Tsar to crush. The armed forces began to mutiny and would not fire on demonstrators. Government buildings were seized by mobs.

- On 12 March the Petrograd Soviet re-emerged. After issuing its Order Number One, which stated that soldiers need not obey orders from the Duma, its control over the soldiers in the city was decisive. On 15 March the Tsar realised that he had no choice but to abdicate.

- A Provisional Government was set up by the Duma. The first prime minister was Prince Lvov. The Provisional Government announced reforms which made Russia a democracy. However, the new government would now have to face exactly the same problems that had led to the overthrow of the Tsar.

Summary Box 3

The First World War and the outbreak of the March Revolution, 1917

- Outbreak of war, August 1914
- Early defeats for Russian armies. Soldiers ill-equipped, badly-led
- Food shortages and unemployment in cities
- Influence of Rasputin over Tsarina. Rasputin's murder, December 1916
- Outbreak of strikes and demonstrations in Petrograd, March 1917
- Re-establishment of Petrograd Soviet and issue of Order Number One to establish its control over armed forces in the city
- Tsar abdicates, 15 March 1917
- Provisional Government set up

What do I Know?

1 Who was Tsar of Russia up to 1917?
2 What was the most important Church in Russia?
3 What change was made to the lives of Russia's peasants in 1861?
4 Which Minister of Finance, appointed in 1892, encouraged the growth of industry?
5 In 1903 the Social Democratic Party split. What did the two groups that split call themselves?
6 What was the Tsarist secret police called?
7 With which country did Russia go to war in 1904?
8 Who led the Bloody Sunday demonstration in 1905?
9 On which battleship was there a famous mutiny during the 1905 revolution?
10 What was the name of the workers' councils which became a leading force in the 1905 revolution?
11 What were the Russian parliaments called?
12 Which Tsarist minister tried to reform Russian agriculture after the 1905 revolution?
13 At which battle in the autumn of 1914 did the Germans halt the Russian attack into East Prussia?
14 What was the Order Number One of the Petrograd Soviet?
15 Who was the first prime minister of the Provisional Government?

My score …

What was the importance of:

- the *zemstvos*
- the Battle of Tsushima
- the October Manifesto
- Rasputin?

The Optional Depth Studies are tested in Section C of Paper 1. On your chosen Depth Study you will have to answer two questions. The first will be a compulsory source-based question. There will be three sources and three sub-questions to answer. The second question will be structured, also consisting of three parts (worth 4, 6 and 10 marks for each part). There will be two of these structured questions, and you choose one.

Here is an example of a structured question on Tsarist rule over Russia up to 1914.

> **(a)** What were the main features of Tsarist rule over Russia?
> **(4 marks)**
>
> **(b)** Why did revolution break out in Russia in January 1905?
> **(6 marks)**
>
> **(c)** How far had the Tsar's regime recovered by 1914 from the effects of the 1905 revolution? Explain your answer.
> **(10 marks)**

Have a go yourself at parts (b) and (c) – here are a couple of students' answers to part (a).

Answer 1

The main features of Tsarist rule were that there was an emperor called the Tsar. He had total power. There was no parliament. To keep opponents in order there was a secret police called the Okhrana.

Answer 2

At the start of the twentieth century Russia was still an autocracy. This means that one man, the Tsar, kept all power in his own hands, and he did not permit any democratic rights, like elections or having a parliament to pass laws. The Russian people had few freedoms. To uphold the autocracy, the Tsar made sure that any opposition was suppressed. No free speech was permitted, newspapers were censored, and a secret police, the Okhrana, arrested anyone suspected of disloyalty to the Tsar.

**Examiner's
Comments:
Answer 1**

4 out of 4

There's really plenty to write about on a topic like this, so the real issue is knowing when to stop! There's only a limited number of marks available, and once you've earned them, anything more is wasted effort! The general guide is that any relevant point will score a mark (and that, up to the total specified, an extra mark can be awarded to each point for additional detail). The difficulty here is deciding on what counts as a 'feature of Tsarist rule'. The examiners are unlikely to be too strict on this, but they will be looking for points which have something to do with how Russia was governed. Very general points about, say, living or working conditions are not going to be rewarded. Looking at this answer, you can see that the writer hasn't wasted much effort on adding details to the four basic points being made.

Answer 2

4 out of 4

You can see straight away that this is a better answer than the first example. There are two broad points – the Tsar's role, and the lack of civil rights – and both are supported by ample additional detail. It's better than the first answer, but you can't get any more than maximum marks!

4.2 How did the Bolsheviks gain power, and how did they consolidate their rule?

Topic Summary

The Provisional Government was weak, and it was undermined continually by the authority of the Petrograd Soviet. The Provisional Government decided to go on with the war but continuing defeats led to mass mutinies in the army. Ongoing food shortages were a problem in the cities. The Bolsheviks promised everything the government could not provide – peace, bread and land for the peasants. They built up their power in the Petrograd Soviet. The Kornilov affair in September 1917 showed how the government relied on the Petrograd Soviet for support. By November the Bolsheviks had sufficient support to stage a revolution. Their Red Guards took over Petrograd. Kerensky fled and the rest of the Provisional Government were captured. The Bolsheviks began to establish a dictatorship. Their opponents organised resistance and a coalition of anti-Bolshevik forces, known as Whites, raised armies to fight the Bolsheviks. Civil war broke out. The Red Army, created by Trotsky, was able to defeat the Whites, but terrible damage was done to Russia. Both sides used terror tactics, there was widespread devastation and starvation, and the economy collapsed. The Kronstadt rising of March 1921 showed how even their own supporters were turning against the Bolsheviks. Lenin (real name, Vladimir Ulyanov) realised that a change of policy was needed. The New Economic Policy was a return to capitalism, which enabled Russia to recover.

What do I Need to Know?

You will need to be able to explain why the Provisional Government was a failure, and why revolutionary groups were able to take over the Petrograd Soviet. You should understand how the Bolsheviks seized power, and know about the main features of their dictatorship. You should be able to explain how and why the Bolsheviks won the civil war, and understand the significance of the Kronstadt rising and the New Economic Policy.

Key Topics

How effectively did the Provisional Government rule Russia in 1917?

- The Provisional Government failed to deal with the three great problems they faced: providing food to the cities, passing land reforms to give land to the peasants, and fighting the First World War.

- Disastrously, the government, headed by Prince Lvov, decided to continue the war. This led to further defeats and mutinies.
- The government was weak and divided. Its authority was undermined by the Petrograd Soviet, which co-ordinated the activities of the national soviet movement and had authority over the working classes.
- The Soviet's Order Number One put the army under its control. This meant that the Soviet was an alternative national government. At first it worked with the Provisional Government, but as it came more under the influence of revolutionaries, it became more of a threat.
- With the help of the Germans, who smuggled him across their country in a sealed train, Lenin returned from exile in Switzerland in April 1917. His April Theses made it clear that the Bolsheviks would overthrow the government if they could. The Bolsheviks, using their slogans 'All Power to the Soviets!' and 'Peace! Bread! Land!', concentrated on winning control of the Petrograd Soviet.
- In July, pro-Bolshevik demonstrators took over Petrograd, but Lenin was not ready to take power. These 'July Days' ended with the government crushing the demonstrations. Kerensky, Minister of War, took over as prime minister of the Provisional Government, and appointed Kornilov as commander-in-chief of Russia's armies.
- In September, the Kornilov Affair showed how much Kerensky's power depended on the Soviet. Kornilov assumed he had Kerensky's support in his attempt to occupy Petrograd and destroy the Soviet. When Kerensky had second thoughts, the Bolsheviks were able to persuade Kornilov's soldiers to abandon the takeover attempt, but without the support of the Red Guards, Kerensky would have been defenceless.
- With the people of Petrograd facing another winter of food shortages, the army disintegrating and the Soviet in the hands of the Bolsheviks, by November 1917 the Provisional Government was on the point of collapse.

Summary Box 1

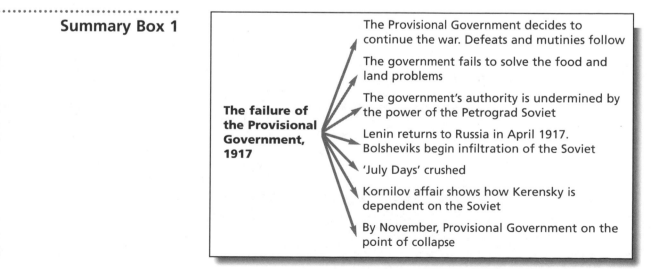

The failure of the Provisional Government, 1917

- The Provisional Government decides to continue the war. Defeats and mutinies follow
- The government fails to solve the food and land problems
- The government's authority is undermined by the power of the Petrograd Soviet
- Lenin returns to Russia in April 1917. Bolsheviks begin infiltration of the Soviet
- 'July Days' crushed
- Kornilov affair shows how Kerensky is dependent on the Soviet
- By November, Provisional Government on the point of collapse

Why were the Bolsheviks able to seize power in November 1917?

- By November 1917 the Provisional Government was unable to defend itself. The only thing delaying a Bolshevik attempt to take power was the influence of other groups in the Soviet, like the Mensheviks.
- On 6 and 7 November Red Guards occupied government buildings throughout Petrograd. There was little violence.
- Kerensky fled. The rest of the government took refuge in the Winter Palace, but were later arrested.
- The Mensheviks and Social Revolutionaries did not resist the Bolshevik takeover. Lenin could now form a Bolshevik government.
- Lenin quickly passed the Decree on Land, which confiscated the estates of landowners and made the land available to the peasants. The Decree on Peace stated that the Bolsheviks would end the war, but this proved difficult. The Germans forced the Bolsheviks to sign the punitive Treaty of Brest-Litovsk in March 1918.
- All large businesses were taken over by the government.
- A secret police, the Cheka, was set up to seek out opponents of the regime.
- Lenin allowed elections to take place, but the Bolsheviks got only 24 per cent of the vote (the Social Revolutionaries got 38 per cent). When the new Constituent Assembly met in January 1918, it would not accept Bolshevik rule so Lenin had it shut down by Bolshevik troops.
- The Bolsheviks had successfully seized power in Russia's main cities, but did not yet control the rest of the country.
- The Bolshevik Party was renamed the Communist Party in March 1918.

Summary Box 2

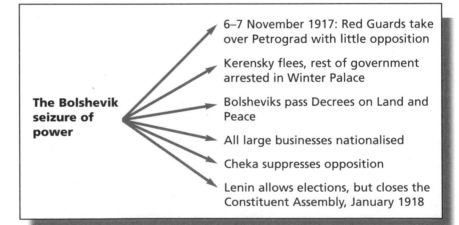

The Bolshevik seizure of power

- 6–7 November 1917: Red Guards take over Petrograd with little opposition
- Kerensky flees, rest of government arrested in Winter Palace
- Bolsheviks pass Decrees on Land and Peace
- All large businesses nationalised
- Cheka suppresses opposition
- Lenin allows elections, but closes the Constituent Assembly, January 1918

Why did the Bolsheviks win the civil war?

- The Bolshevik's opponents, known as the Whites, consisted of many different groups: monarchists, middle-class liberals, landowners, Mensheviks, and even foreign powers who intervened because of their fear of the Bolshevik regime.
- The Whites were not united in their aims: they had no single command and they were geographically scattered. Their leaders, such as Kolchak, Denikin and Yudenich, worked independently of one another.
- The Bolsheviks held a central position – including Russia's two greatest cities, they were united and had the simple aim of survival.
- Trotsky created the Red Army. His energy and ruthlessness made him the ideal war leader. He used fierce discipline and travelled around by train encouraging his troops.
- The Bolsheviks introduced War Communism to make sure the army had enough supplies. All aspects of the economy were taken over by the government. The Cheka went out into the countryside to seize peasants' grain supplies.
- The Cheka launched a 'Red Terror' to intimidate the Bolsheviks' opponents. Thousands were arrested and executed. Amongst the victims were the Tsar and his family, imprisoned at Ekaterinburg in the Urals, then murdered in July 1918.
- The civil war was exceptionally brutal. Both sides committed atrocities. Gradually the Red Army gained the upper hand. By 1920 fighting came to an end with the Red Army victorious.
- The Russian economy was in ruins. The people had suffered terribly and there was widespread starvation. The Bolshevik regime had become a cruel dictatorship. Even its supporters had come to hate it. In March 1921 the sailors of the Kronstadt naval base mutinied and demanded an end to dictatorship.
- The Kronstadt sailors had been supporters of the Bolsheviks. Their mutiny was crushed with much bloodshed, but it was a warning to Lenin that he must change policy.

Summary Box 3

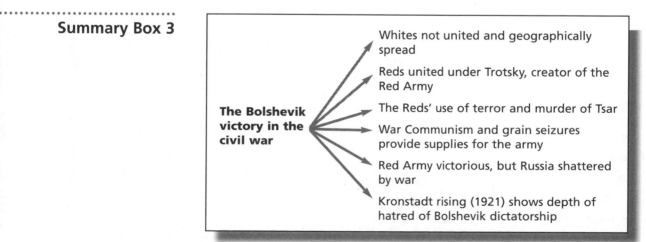

The Bolshevik victory in the civil war

- Whites not united and geographically spread
- Reds united under Trotsky, creator of the Red Army
- The Reds' use of terror and murder of Tsar
- War Communism and grain seizures provide supplies for the army
- Red Army victorious, but Russia shattered by war
- Kronstadt rising (1921) shows depth of hatred of Bolshevik dictatorship

How far was the New Economic Policy a success?

- Lenin knew that the peasants had to be given incentives to produce more food. Grain seizures had produced only starvation; government control had to be relaxed.

- In 1921 Lenin announced the New Economic Policy (NEP), a return to the ideas of capitalism. Big industries would stay in state hands, but small businesses and agriculture would be put back into private hands. People could sell their goods for a profit.

- Almost immediately the economy started to recover. Food appeared in the shops, and thousands of small businesses sprang up. Production rapidly increased.

- By 1927 production had returned to pre-First World War levels.

- However, the NEP was criticised by many communists as a betrayal. Others were worried that Russia was recovering too slowly and that, under the NEP, it would never be possible to make Russia a modern industrial power.

What do I Know?

1 Who replaced Lvov as prime minister in July 1917?

2 Give one of the propaganda slogans used by the Bolsheviks during 1917.

3 What was Lenin's real name?

4 Where was Lenin in exile at the beginning of 1917?

5 How did Lenin get back to Russia after the March revolution?

6 Who was appointed commander-in-chief of Russia's armies in July 1917?

7 Where did members of the Provisional Government take refuge during the November revolution?

8 Which two decrees did the Bolsheviks issue on taking power?

9 Name the peace treaty Russia signed with Germany in March 1918.

10 What was the name of the Bolshevik secret police?

11 What happened to the Constituent Assembly when it met in January 1918?

12 Name one of the White generals in the civil war.

13 Who created the Red Army?

14 Who was held under arrest until July 1918 in Ekaterinburg in the Ural Mountains?

15 Where did an uprising against the Bolshevik dictatorship occur in March 1921?

My score …

What was the importance of:

- the April Theses
- the 'July Days'
- the Kornilov affair
- War Communism?

Exam Type Question

The Optional Depth Studies are tested in Section C of Paper 1. On your chosen Depth Study you will have to answer two questions. The first will be a compulsory source-based question. There will be three sources and three sub-questions to answer. The second question will be structured, also consisting of three parts (worth 4, 6 and 10 marks for each part). There will be two of these structured questions, and you choose one.

Here is an example of a structured question on the Bolshevik seizure of power.

(a) What were the main problems the Provisional Government faced on taking over from the Tsar? **(4 marks)**

(b) Why were the Bolsheviks able to seize power in November 1917? **(6 marks)**

(c) 'The most important reason the Bolsheviks were able to defeat the White armies in the civil war was the Whites had no single leader.' Do you agree with this statement? Explain your answer. **(10 marks)**

Have a go yourself at parts (a) and (c) – here are a couple of students' answers to part (b).

Answer 1

By November 1917 the Provisional Government was so weak that it no longer had any supporters. The food problem hadn't been solved and people in the cities faced starvation again. The Provisional Government hadn't even held the elections that were promised so that a proper government could be chosen. Its decision to continue the war had brought disaster. The troops would not fight and there were mass desertions. Those soldiers that stayed in the army were no longer loyal. So this is why the Bolsheviks were able to seize power in November 1917.

Answer 2

The Bolsheviks planned to takeover. From the moment Lenin got back to Petrograd in April 1917 they had worked hard to gain control of the Soviet, because they knew that this would give them control over Petrograd. By November 1917 they had achieved this and were ready to strike against the Provisional Government. The Bolsheviks had the support of the people because they promised all the things the government had not provided – peace, bread and land. The moment the Red Guards started occupying government buildings, it was clear that the government would not resist. Kerensky fled and the rest gave up without a fight. The Bolsheviks were able to take over because they were well organised, and the government was rotten and ready to collapse.

Examiner's Comments: Answer 1

5 out of 6

In part (b) questions you earn marks for giving reasons and explaining them – *identifying* reasons will only get you about half of the marks. If you want to do well, you will also have to *explain* the reasons. Of course, the reasons also have to be relevant. The problem with the reasons given in this answer is that they seem to be answering a different question, such as 'Why was the Provisional Government weak?' They certainly don't explain why the Bolsheviks were able to seize power, in fact they seem to ignore the Bolsheviks altogether. However, being charitable, the examiner would probably be happy to credit these as background reasons – they certainly help explain why a takeover by *someone* was possible. Two reasons – the Provisional Government's loss of support and its decision to continue the war – are explained.

Answer 2

6 out of 6

This is a much more direct approach which focuses well on what it was about the Bolsheviks that enabled them to seize power. There are three reasons given, all explained.

4.3 How did Stalin gain and hold on to power?

Topic Summary

Lenin's death in 1924 sparked off a struggle for power. The main contenders to take over were Trotsky and the secretive outsider from Georgia, Stalin. The struggle was not resolved for several years, but eventually Stalin emerged as undisputed leader. Worried by the prospect that his opponents might still try to turn against him, Stalin decided to get rid of them. The murder of Kirov in 1934 gave Stalin the chance to launch the purges, during which his enemies were arrested, accused of imaginary crimes, and put on trial. Many were executed. The purges saw the execution of almost all the 'Old Bolsheviks'. In 1936 Stalin extended the purges to all branches of society by starting the 'Great Terror': the secret police crushed any opposition; hundreds of thousands of people were executed, and millions were imprisoned; everyone lived in fear of arrest. Stalin's terror tactics were backed up by endless propaganda. It was impossible for people to think for themselves – radio, films, newspapers, posters – everything was controlled by the government. Stalin was presented in this propaganda as the greatest genius of the age. By 1941 he had achieved almost total power over the Soviet Union.

What do I Need to Know?

You will need to explain why Stalin, and not Trotsky, was able to emerge as Lenin's successor. You should know what the purges were, and why Stalin used them. You should understand the impact that Stalin's use of terror had on the Soviet Union, and know about the other methods he used to control the Soviet people. You will have to assess the extent of Stalin's control over the Soviet Union by 1941.

Key Topics

Why did Stalin, and not Trotsky, emerge as Lenin's successor?

- For the last year of his life, following three serious strokes, Lenin was an invalid, playing no active role in running the country. In January 1924 he died. His death set off a struggle to become his successor, which was not resolved for several years.
- The two main contenders were Trotsky and Stalin (the name means 'Man of Steel'). Trotsky seemed to be the better candidate – organiser of the November Revolution and creator of the Red Army, but he was mistrusted by his colleagues. Stalin was better placed. As General Secretary of the Communist Party he had placed his supporters in many of the top Party posts.

- Trotsky's ideas seemed too extreme to many communists. He wanted 'permanent revolution' and opposed the introduction of the NEP. Stalin seemed to offer a quieter life. His policy was 'socialism in one country'.
- Lenin warned against Stalin in his 'political will'. He said Stalin had concentrated too much power in his own hands. This warning was ignored because of the jealousy most communist leaders felt for Trotsky.
- Stalin, Zinoviev and Kamenev accused Trotsky of trying to split the Communist Party and take power himself. In 1925 Trotsky lost his position as Minister of War, then in 1926 he was removed from the Politburo. Finally, in 1929, he was forced into exile in Mexico.
- Having dealt with Trotsky, Stalin turned on Zinoviev and Kamenev. He accused them of working with Trotsky's supporters in a 'United Opposition', and had them sacked.
- By 1928 Stalin had emerged as leader of the Soviet Union, but he was still deeply suspicious of his opponents.

Summary Box 1

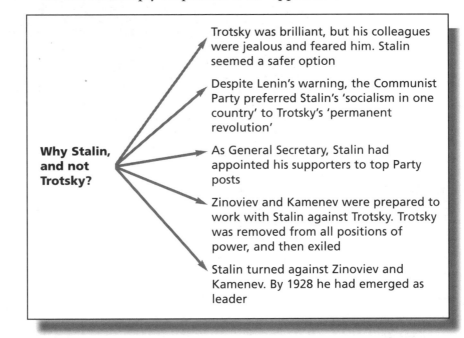

Why Stalin, and not Trotsky?

Trotsky was brilliant, but his colleagues were jealous and feared him. Stalin seemed a safer option

Despite Lenin's warning, the Communist Party preferred Stalin's 'socialism in one country' to Trotsky's 'permanent revolution'

As General Secretary, Stalin had appointed his supporters to top Party posts

Zinoviev and Kamenev were prepared to work with Stalin against Trotsky. Trotsky was removed from all positions of power, and then exiled

Stalin turned against Zinoviev and Kamenev. By 1928 he had emerged as leader

Why did Stalin launch the purges?

- The struggle for power had made it obvious that the communist leadership disagreed about many matters.
- Stalin was not prepared to accept challenges to his authority. He planned a purge of the top Party membership to get rid of anyone he did not trust. In 1934, the murder of the Leningrad Communist Party boss, Kirov, gave him his chance. Stalin had Zinoviev, Kamenev and others arrested and accused of the murder. In 1935 they were tried and sentenced to long periods of imprisonment.

- This was not enough for Stalin. The following year he started the 'Great Terror' by having Zinoviev and Kamenev tried as foreign spies. They were found guilty and shot. The 'show trials' of dozens of top communists followed. The NKVD (secret police) had hundreds of thousands of people murdered, and millions imprisoned. When Yagoda, head of the NKVD, failed to arrange enough arrests, he was replaced by the ruthless Yezhov.

- The purges of the top ranks of the armed forces were so severe that, when Germany invaded in 1941, the Soviet Union lacked the experienced officers it needed to organise effective resistance.

- By 1938 the terror was affecting the economy. So many top managers, officials, supervisors, engineers and scientists had disappeared that production fell. Stalin called an end to the terror. As a final twist he turned against the NKVD and had most of its top officers, including its head, Yezhov, arrested and shot.

- In 1940 NKVD agents finally caught up with Trotsky who was in exile in Mexico, and he was murdered by them.

What methods did Stalin use to control the Soviet Union?

- Stalin was leader of a totalitarian state. There were no human rights. People could be arrested, imprisoned and murdered without trial. They could just disappear and nobody would ever know what happened to them. Millions of innocent people suffered. It wasn't necessary to have done anything wrong; suspicion of being disloyal was enough.

- Informers were everywhere. Children were even encouraged to inform on their own parents. Pavlik Morozov, a peasant boy who informed on his father for hoarding grain, was used as an example to follow. Few people dared to utter criticism of Stalin.

- Millions of people were imprisoned in labour camps. By 1939 there were around 3 million people in the camps. They were kept in terrible conditions, given little food, and forced to work through the cold of the Russian winter. Around 200,000 died in building the White Sea Canal.

- Stalin made great use of propaganda. Radio, films and newspapers were all controlled by the state. Schools taught communist versions of history and science. The state told people what to think; even artists had to do what the state told them.

- Because the truth of what was happening was hidden, many Soviet citizens believed the propaganda. They were told that Stalin was a great genius who would look after them. Stalin's image was everywhere. A cult of Stalin's personality developed. In one speech, Stalin was called 'Leader of Genius of the Proletarian Revolution' and 'Supreme Genius of Humanity'. One of the world's most evil tyrants was loved by many of the people he ruled.

- Stalin's dictatorship was as complete as he could make it. Even so, there were limits to this power. In a country the size of the Soviet Union it was impossible to control all aspects of people's daily lives. There was petty crime, and the divorce and abortion rates rose fast, despite official disapproval.

Summary Box 2

How did Stalin control the Soviet Union?

- 1934: Murder of Kirov starts the purges
- Zinoviev and Kamenev tried and imprisoned
- 1936: 'show trials' of Old Bolsheviks
- The Great Terror starts. Hundreds of thousands purged in all walks of life
- NKVD under Yezhov used to carry out terror policy
- Millions imprisoned in labour camps
- Use of propaganda encourages 'cult of personality'

What do I Know?

1. In what year did Lenin die?
2. What was the main point made in Lenin's 'political will'?
3. What did the name 'Stalin' mean?
4. What part of the Soviet Union did Stalin come from?
5. What Party position had Stalin held that enabled him to place his supporters in important posts?
6. What was Trotsky's policy for the future development of communism?
7. What position did Trotsky lose in January 1925?
8. What happened to Trotsky in 1929?
9. Which two important communists supported Stalin in the struggle against Trotsky?
10. Whose murder in 1934 sparked off the purges?
11. Who was leader of the NKVD after Yagoda was sacked?
12. Who was Pavlik Morozov?
13. Roughly how many people were imprisoned in Stalin's labour camps by 1939?
14. Which project was built by convict labour and cost nearly 200,000 prisoners' lives?
15. Who was called 'Leader of Genius of the Proletarian Revolution' and 'Supreme Genius of Humanity'?

My score …

What was the importance of:

- the 'United Opposition'
- the 'show trials'
- the NKVD
- the cult of personality?

The Optional Depth Studies are tested in Section C of Paper 1. On your chosen Depth Study you will have to answer two questions. The first will be a compulsory source-based question. There will be three sources and three sub-questions to answer. The source-based question carries 20 marks in total, with the three parts each being worth 6, 7 and 7 marks, though not necessarily in that order. Although the questions are source-based and test source-handling skills, they also require you to use your knowledge.

The second question will be structured, also consisting of three parts (worth 4, 6 and 10 marks for each part). There will be two of these structured questions, and you choose one.

Take a look at the following source-based example. Study the sources carefully, and then answer the questions which follow.

Source A

▲ **A French poster of Stalin from the 1930s.**

Source B

I was in love with that man, and I love him still. The day he died I wept like a baby. I loved him for his mind, his logic, his manliness, and especially his courage. He was the one person great enough to keep the Soviet Union together after Lenin's death. It was for him that we worked and sacrificed and died. He was a genius of his time.

▲ **A former manager of a collective farm remembering Stalin in 1967.**

Source C

▲ **A cartoon published in France in 1936 by Russian exiles about new seating arrangements in the Soviet parliament.**

(a) Study Source A.
Do you think this cartoon was published by supporters or by opponents of Stalin? Use the source and your knowledge to explain your answer. **(6 marks)**

(b) Study Source B.
Can you explain why this man loved Stalin so much? Use the source and your own knowledge to explain your answer. **(7 marks)**

(c) Study Source C.
Why do you think Russian exiles published this cartoon in 1936? Use the source and your knowledge to explain your answer. **(7 marks)**

Have a go yourself at parts (a) and (c) – here are a couple of students' answers to part (b).

Answer 1

> I think this man loved Stalin because he believed he was a great man. He says that only Stalin was great enough to hold the Soviet Union together when Lenin died. He loved him because he was a genius.

Answer 2

> This man loved Stalin so much because of the cult of personality. Soviet citizens had to live with constant propaganda. It was impossible for them to know the truth of what was going on, so they ended up believing what they were told. The propaganda said Stalin was a genius, and that's what this man says, even though he's speaking many years after Stalin's death. He believed that he loved Stalin, but really what he loved was the image of Stalin.

Examiner's Comments: Answer 1

3 out of 7

This answer is limited by the fact that it only uses the source – the reasons that it gives for why the man loved Stalin are all taken from the source. In answering this question it would be possible to accept the accuracy of what the source says, and to back it up with reference to your own knowledge of Stalin's achievements (alternatively, answer 2 gives another approach). For example, Stalin may have been an evil monster, but he gave the impression of being a strong and great leader. However, the answer does not attempt this and just sticks to the source alone.

Answer 2

7 out of 7

This answer takes the other possible route to using background knowledge. That is, it rejects the accuracy of what the man says as being merely the result of brainwashing. By referring to the cult of personality, the answer effectively explains why the man holds this opinion. The writer makes a good point in saying that it was really an image of Stalin that the man loved, not Stalin himself. It is important here to make more than a passing reference to 'propaganda' by explaining why the propaganda made the man love Stalin.

4.4 What was the impact of Stalin's economic policies?

Topic Summary

Stalin was determined to modernise the Soviet Union, and to do it quickly. He believed that, if the Soviet Union did not catch up with the West, the capitalist nations would one day destroy it. His method of industrialisation was through state planning and central control of the economy. The state created a series of Five-Year Plans which laid down production targets and decided on industrial priorities. From 1928 these plans transformed the Soviet Union into an industrial power. To pay for this development, agriculture also had to modernise. Stalin needed to sell grain in order to buy the machinery that industry required. While the land was in the peasants' hands, he could not do this, so he decided to collectivise agriculture. The land would be owned by the state, and the peasants would work for wages. The peasants resisted this change; so, with great brutality, collectivisation was forced on them. Stalin paid a high price for the change. He got control of agriculture, but production never recovered. Soviet society under Stalin consisted of three broad groups: the peasants resentfully working on collective farms; industrial workers who enjoyed a gradually improving standard of living; and the social elite who enjoyed a range of perks. In theory, women enjoyed equality with men, though in practice the traditional male dominance of society continued. The many ethnic minorities were put under pressure to conform and to abandon their traditions by Stalin's policy of Russification.

What do I Need to Know?

You will need to know how and why Stalin modernised the Soviet Union. You must understand how the Five-Year Plans worked, and what the impact of the plans was on the Soviet people. You should know why agriculture also had to be modernised, and why Stalin introduced collectivisation. You should be able to explain why the peasants resisted these changes and what the effects of this were, both on the peasants themselves and on agriculture in general. You will need to know about the social structure of the Soviet Union under Stalin, and be aware of the differing experiences of women and ethnic minorities.

Key Topics

Why did Stalin introduce the Five-Year Plans?

- In the 1920s, the Soviet Union was still a backward, rural country by Western standards. Stalin saw modernisation as a matter of life or death. But he did not believe the NEP could modernise the country quickly enough.

- Gosplan, the state planning bureau, was given the task of drawing up the Five-Year Plans.
- The plans would decide targets for industrial production, and central control of the economy would ensure that resources were available to achieve the targets.
- The first Five-Year Plan was launched in 1928. It focused on heavy industry. Huge projects were started and tough targets were set. It was a time of enormous achievements and hardships.
- The second Five-Year Plan started in 1933. It concentrated on transport and production of machinery. There was more production of consumer goods. It was a less frantic period than the first Plan.
- The third Five-Year Plan began in 1938. It was interrupted by the outbreak of war in 1941. More and more investment was transferred into defence-related industries. This plan was also affected badly by the purges, which held back production.
- The Five-Year Plans made the Soviet Union the second greatest industrial power in the world. Factories and mines, dams, canals, and new towns sprang up all over the Soviet Union.
- The workers were encouraged by endless propaganda. The Stakhanovite movement, named after Stakhanov, the miner who cut 102 tons of coal in six hours, urged workers to produce more and more.
- However, there were inevitable problems. The use of targets produced a concentration of quantity at the expense of quality. There were not enough skilled workers, a situation only worsened by the purges. Workers had no rights and were subjected to tough discipline. Safety standards were poor.
- It is impossible to know exactly how successful the Five-Year Plans were. Any Soviet figures are unreliable. The Soviet Union was certainly transformed, but the real debate is whether this could have been achieved by other, less drastic methods.

Summary Box 1

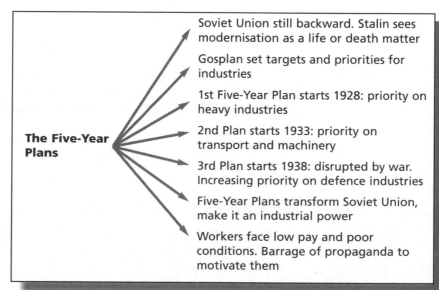

The Five-Year Plans

- Soviet Union still backward. Stalin sees modernisation as a life or death matter
- Gosplan set targets and priorities for industries
- 1st Five-Year Plan starts 1928: priority on heavy industries
- 2nd Plan starts 1933: priority on transport and machinery
- 3rd Plan starts 1938: disrupted by war. Increasing priority on defence industries
- Five-Year Plans transform Soviet Union, make it an industrial power
- Workers face low pay and poor conditions. Barrage of propaganda to motivate them

Why did Stalin introduce collectivisation?

- Soviet agriculture still used traditional, inefficient methods. To increase production, it would have to be modernised.
- Stalin had two reasons for wanting to take agriculture into state hands. First, he needed to sell grain to earn hard currency to invest in industry. Second, if the peasants kept control of grain sales, they would want to keep the price high. Stalin wanted cheap food for the industrial workers so he could keep wages low.
- Stalin wanted to set up collective farms. The land would be owned by the state, and the peasants would work for wages.
- The peasants resisted these changes. Stalin claimed it was only the greedy, rich peasants (known as 'kulaks') who resisted. In reality, it was almost everyone. To force them to accept, Stalin sent soldiers into the countryside. They seized the grain and took the peasants' farms from them.
- The peasants responded by killing all their livestock and eating all their food. Soon there was famine. Around 5 million died of starvation in the Ukraine during 1932–3.
- Some modernisation did occur on the collective farms, known as *kolkhoz*. Machine tractor stations were set up, new techniques and crops were adopted.
- Stalin controlled agriculture, but production did not recover. Given the fall in production and the costs of collectivisation, Stalin would probably have had more food for the industrial workers and hard cash to invest if he had left agriculture alone.

Summary Box 2

Collectivisation

- Soviet agriculture inefficient and backward
- Stalin wants collectivisation to control grain sales – he needs hard currency for industry and cheap food for the workers
- Peasants resist collectivisation
- Stalin uses force against them. Millions die in famines which follow
- Some modernisation follows, but production never recovers

How were the Soviet people affected by these changes?

- The Soviet Union contained many different national groups. At first they were allowed to retain their own customs. However, after 1934 Stalin introduced a policy of Russification. Russian became a compulsory subject at school, Russian people were encouraged to migrate into non-Russian areas, and the ethnic minorities were encouraged to see themselves as Soviet citizens. Ethnic minority leaders became a particular target of the purges.

- The Revolution claimed to have given women equality with men. However, the Soviet Union remained male-dominated. Soviet women were expected to work, and had a much wider range of work open to them than women in Western countries. But working women were also expected to do all the domestic chores. Medals were awarded to women who had more than 10 children.
- Soviet society consisted of three broad groups: the peasants, the industrial workers, and the social elite.
- The peasants resented collectivisation and lived pretty miserable lives. They were allowed small private plots of land to work on; without these they would have found it hard even to survive.
- The industrial workers experienced slightly improving conditions during the 1930s. Wages remained low but more people were working, so families could afford a few basic consumer goods. Free education and medicine were available to most workers.
- The social elite consisted of managers, Party bosses and scientists. They had a higher standard of living with many perks, like holidays, better housing and special shops. They were resented by the other classes and this made them easy targets for informers. Many suffered in the purges.

What do I Know?

What was the importance of:
- Gosplan
- the Stakhanovites
- the kulaks
- Russification?

1. Name the planning bureau that had the task of drawing up the Five-Year Plans.
2. When was the first Five-Year Plan launched?
3. What was the priority set for the first Five-Year Plan?
4. Why was the third Five-Year Plan not completed?
5. Name the coal miner who was used as an example to encourage other workers to increase production.
6. What were kulaks?
7. In which part of the Soviet Union did around 5 million peasants die of starvation in 1932–3?
8. What were *kolkhoz*?
9. What policy did Stalin apply to ethnic minorities after 1934?
10. How were women encouraged to have large numbers of children?

My score ...

Exam Type Question

The Optional Depth Studies are tested in Section C of Paper 1. On your chosen Depth Study you will have to answer two questions. The first will be a compulsory source-based question. There will be three sources and three sub-questions to answer. The second question will be structured, also consisting of three parts (worth 4, 6 and 10 marks for each part). There will be two of these structured questions, and you choose one.

Here is an example of a structured question on Stalin's economic policies.

> **(a)** What were the Five-Year Plans? **(4 marks)**
>
> **(b)** Explain why Stalin thought it so important to modernise the Soviet Union. **(6 marks)**
>
> **(c)** 'Stalin's collectivisation of agriculture was a complete disaster.' Do you agree with this statement? Explain your answer. **(10 marks)**

Have a go yourself at parts (a) and (b) – here are a couple of students' answers to part (c).

Answer 1

Collectivisation was a disaster because so many peasants died. They did not want to work for the state, so they refused to go onto collectives. Then the army forced them. When this happened other peasants knew they would lose everything, so they just ate all the food they had stored, killed all their animals and ate them too. Then there was no food, so famine broke out. Millions of people starved because of this. And there wasn't any point to it because even when they were forced to work on collectives, nobody wanted to work hard so production just declined. All in all it was pretty pointless and just made matters worse.

Answer 2

Whether or not collectivisation was a disaster depends on which way you look at it. It was a disaster for the peasants. They lost their land, they were forced to work on collectives when they didn't want to, and millions of them were deliberately starved to death by Stalin. It wasn't good for production, because this fell sharply, and Soviet agriculture never really recovered. It wasn't even effective in making the peasants work together. Not many state farms were set up, and on the kolkhoz the peasants were only really motivated to work on their own small plots. However, none of this is what collectivisation was really about. The real issue is whether Stalin achieved his aims or not. He needed control of grain production, so that grain sales could finance industrialisation. Collectivisation gave him this control, so as far as Stalin was concerned, it served its purpose. In this sense it was not a disaster. However, nowadays historians think that it didn't really achieve what he wanted, because the costs of collectivisation were higher than anything he gained from it. If it's true that he would have got more hard currency and cheaper food from leaving things alone, then collectivisation certainly was a disaster!

Examiner's Comments: Answer 1

6 out of 10

By now you should be aware that the trick in part (c) questions is to look at *both sides* of the argument. No matter how detailed your answer, if it simply accepts the given statement and doesn't consider other opinions then it's not going to get a top mark. This answer is actually quite a good explanation of why collectivisation can be seen as a disaster, but there's not a hint of an alternative view.

Answer 2

10 out of 10

This answer obviously has what Answer 1 lacks. It shows that whether or not collectivisation was a disaster is mainly a matter of perspective – there are arguments on both sides. This, in itself, would be enough to get eight or nine marks, but the answer goes one better by weighing up the arguments to reach a reasoned conclusion: making the point that maybe Stalin would have achieved his aims more effectively had he not collectivised.

5 The USA 1919–41

5.1 How far did the US economy boom in the 1920s?

Topic Summary

During the 1920s the production of US industry increased by around 50 per cent. The USA's natural wealth, low taxes and, above all, new consumer industries, such as electrical goods and automobiles, combined to produce an economic boom. The automobile industry, for example, showed how consumer goods could be mass-produced cheaply in order to increase sales. During the 1920s ownership of a motor car became a possibility for ordinary workers, thanks mainly to Henry Ford's 'Model T'. The car transformed people's social lives, liberating them from their own immediate locality and opening the country up to them. However, despite the boom, not all industries benefited. Traditional heavy industries had less opportunity for expansion, and agriculture suffered badly from overproduction and low prices. Not all workers shared in the growing prosperity. Farm workers, of whom most in the South were black, often lived below the poverty line.

What do I Need to Know?

You will need to explain the factors on which the economic boom depended, in particular, the impact of the automobile industry and the principle of mass production. You should be aware that not all industries benefited from the boom, and be able to explain why. You should know about the problems affecting agriculture and understand that, despite the boom, the majority of Americans were still poor, with minority groups, such as blacks and native Americans, having the worst prospects of all.

Key Topics

On what factors was the economic boom based?

By the end of the First World War, the USA was the richest country in the world. Although it entered the war in 1917, it experienced none of the physical destruction that Europe suffered. Rather, its industries were boosted by war production. By 1920, government figures showed that more than half of the population now lived in towns. During the 1920s the US economy boomed. There were several factors which helped bring the boom about:

- The emergence of a range of new industries – electrical goods, automobiles, chemicals. Consumer goods like radios, washing machines and fridges became widely available.

- The use of assembly-line mass-production techniques, as pioneered by Henry Ford, made goods cheaper so that more people could afford them.
- Wages went up so that people had more to spend.
- The governments of the 1920s followed economic policies which boosted industry. Andrew Mellon, Secretary to the Treasury, cut taxes so that consumers would spend more and raised tariffs (taxes on trade) on imported goods. The Fordney-McCumber Tariff Act of 1922 raised tariffs higher than ever before. President Coolidge said, 'The business of America is business'.
- Selling techniques improved. Hire purchase became widely available so that consumers could buy goods on credit. Mail order catalogues, like the popular Sears Roebuck catalogue, made goods available to people throughout the country.
- The Republican governments, like businessmen, were hostile towards trade unions. Employers often used violence against workers who tried to unionise.
- The automobile industry was the most important of all, and employed the most workers. Henry Ford's 'Model T' made cars widely available. The cars of two other giant companies, General Motors and Chrysler, were almost as popular. The growth of the industry had enormous effects on the economy as a whole, boosting employment in construction, service industries like hotels and restaurants, and the oil industry, as well as industries making components for the cars themselves.
- The automobile had significant social consequences. Rural life became less isolated, people could live in suburbs and drive to work, car owners could take touring holidays, and so on.

Summary Box 1

Causes of the 1920s boom

- USA rich in natural resources
- New industries developing: electrical goods, automobiles, chemicals
- Mass production made goods cheaper, so more people could afford to buy them
- Government followed policies friendly to industry: cut taxes and imposed tariffs on imports
- Development of hire purchase and catalogue selling

Why did some industries prosper while others did not?

- The boom was based mainly on new industries. There was a new and growing demand for the goods made by these industries. Increased wealth meant that people could afford such consumer goods. Construction also boomed, with the world's highest skyscraper, the Empire State Building in New York, complete in 1931.

- However, in long-established traditional industries consumer demand did not grow so fast. The markets for these goods were already established, and the products were not new and exciting.
- Some traditional industries faced competition from new industries. The textile industry, based in the north-east of the country, was threatened by the invention of man-made fibres. Coal mines closed as people switched to electricity or oil for heating.

Why did agriculture not share in the prosperity?

- The basic problem with agriculture was overproduction. The USA could not eat all the food it produced, and neither could it export enough of the surplus. As a result, prices fell sharply.
- This meant that farmers' incomes also fell. Many farmers had to borrow from banks in the hope of better times to come. When they couldn't repay their loans, their farms were seized.
- Rural areas did not benefit from the boom. Few farms had basic amenities like electricity or mains water.
- The south was worst affected. Reliance on single crops like cotton and tobacco made the area more vulnerable to falling prices. Also, crops were often lost to pests like the boll-weevil.
- Some areas of agriculture did a little better. Greater prosperity meant increasing demand for fresh vegetables and fruit. Farmers in areas where these were produced earned much more.

Did all Americans benefit from the boom?

- Although the USA became richer during the 1920s, this increase in wealth was not shared equally. The rich and middle classes got richer, and the wages of industrial workers increased slightly, but the poor remained poor. By 1929 around 60 per cent of all families still lived below the poverty line.
- Some areas of the country prospered more than others. The industrial areas of the north and west did well, but the agricultural areas of the south and the Great Plains were in depression.
- Racial minorities suffered discrimination in employment. During the First World War many black people had moved from the south to look for work in the industrial cities of the north. After the war there was greater competition for jobs, which led to tension and race riots.
- Urban blacks were, however, better off than the black agricultural workers of the south, who were often employed as sharecroppers – they were not paid anything at all, but worked for a proportion of the crop.
- The most disadvantaged group of all was the Native Americans, who were confined to reservations, often on land so poor that it was impossible to make a living from it.

Summary Box 2

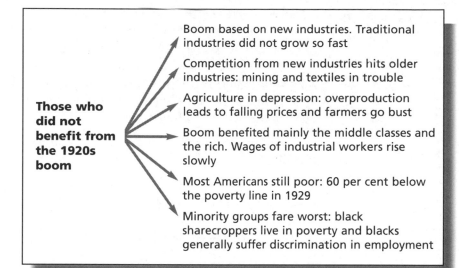

Those who did not benefit from the 1920s boom

- Boom based on new industries. Traditional industries did not grow so fast
- Competition from new industries hits older industries: mining and textiles in trouble
- Agriculture in depression: overproduction leads to falling prices and farmers go bust
- Boom benefited mainly the middle classes and the rich. Wages of industrial workers rise slowly
- Most Americans still poor: 60 per cent below the poverty line in 1929
- Minority groups fare worst: black sharecroppers live in poverty and blacks generally suffer discrimination in employment

What do I Know?

1 Name one of the household electrical goods that became generally available during the 1920s.

2 In which year did government figures first show more people living in towns than in the country?

3 What major change in production techniques was made by Henry Ford?

4 What was Ford's most famous automobile?

5 Who said, 'The business of America is business'?

6 Who was the US Secretary to the Treasury during the 1920s?

7 What are tariffs?

8 Which was the most popular mail order catalogue of the 1920s?

9 Which industry employed the most workers?

10 What were the three firms that dominated the US automobile industry?

11 What was the highest building in the world, completed in 1931?

12 What was a boll-weevil?

13 Roughly what proportion of the US population lived in poverty in the 1920s?

14 What was 'sharecropping'?

15 What were the two most important agricultural crops of the southern states?

My score …

What was the importance of:

- the assembly line
- the Fordney-McCumber Tariff Act (1922)
- hire purchase
- mass ownership of automobiles?

133

**Exam Type
Question**

The Optional Depth Studies are tested in Section C of Paper 1. On your chosen Depth Study you will have to answer two questions. The first will be a compulsory source-based question. There will be three sources and three sub-questions to answer. The second question will be structured, also consisting of three parts (worth 4, 6 and 10 marks for each part). There will be two of these structured questions, and you choose one.

Here is an example of a structured question on the US economy in the 1920s.

(a) What problems did US agriculture face during the 1920s?
(4 marks)

(b) Explain why the US economy boomed during the 1920s.
(6 marks)

(c) How far did the boom of the 1920s benefit the US people? Explain your answer. **(10 marks)**

Have a go yourself at parts (b) and (c) – here are a couple of students' answers to part (a).

Answer 1

Agriculture was depressed in the 1920s. Farmers could not grow enough food and so they were very poor. They did not have their own land, and so they had to work for other people who did not pay them and just gave them food. The crops all got eaten by insects.

Answer 2

The basic problem facing agriculture in the 1920s was that farmers were too efficient. They could grow more than the country needed but overproducing had the effect of pushing down prices. If prices were low, then farmers could not earn enough to live. Many of the farmers borrowed money using their farm as security, but when prices stayed low they couldn't pay back the loan so they lost their farm to the bank. Between 1920 and 1929 the proportion of families that were farmers fell from one-third of the population to one-quarter. This shows how hard it was to make a living out of agriculture.

**Examiner's
Comments:
Answer 1**

2 out of 4
Weaker answers are often like this. They contain material that is wrong mixed in with bits and pieces of information that show some basic knowledge. Marks are never deducted for what a student gets wrong; they are earned by what the student gets right. So this

answer gets some credit, but not much. It's true that agriculture was depressed and that many farmers were poor. The references to farmers not growing enough food and not owning their own land are mistakes – the student is confusing sharecropping with farming in general. Finally, it's true that pests were a serious problem with certain crops. These points are made in a vague and imprecise manner, without demonstrating any specific knowledge.

Answer 2

4 out of 4

On the basis that an answer will score a mark for each relevant point (or a mark for a relevant point and a bonus mark for additional information on that point), this will score all four marks. It's accurate and relevant, and point follows point: overproduction, low prices, low earnings, debt, repossessions, families leaving the land. It also avoids the trap of being too long and wasting time. Don't spend ages answering part (a) questions only to run out of time when answering part (c), which is worth more marks.

5.2   How far did US society change in the 1920s?

During the 1920s the USA was a society of sharp contrasts. The popular image is of the 'Roaring Twenties' or the 'Jazz Age' – a time of fun, parties, dance crazes like the Charleston and liberated young women known as 'flappers'. People did have more leisure, and more money to spend. They were more free to enjoy themselves. Sport developed as mass entertainment, cinema audiences doubled in a decade, and radio ownership became almost universal. Yet the USA was also a troubled and intolerant society. The backlash from the 'Red Scare' of the post-war years was directed mainly at recent immigrants. Black Americans suffered discrimination and violence, and the growth of the Ku Klux Klan indicated that extreme racist views were still widely held by whites. The attempt to ban alcohol – prohibition – turned out to be a failure, putting huge revenues into the hands of gangsters and unleashing a crime wave. The 'Monkey Trial' of 1925 showed how traditional values were being challenged by new ideas and values. Another major change was seen in the lives now led by women: many more women went out to work, being liberated from traditional roles as mothers and housewives by the widespread availability of contraception and labour-saving devices.

What do I Need to Know?

You will need to be aware of the main characteristics of the 'Roaring Twenties': developments in mass entertainment such as the cinema, sport, music, and radio. You should know of the intolerance in US society, such as the causes and effects of the 'Red Scare', and the discrimination against black Americans. You will need to understand why prohibition was introduced, and what the impact of this was on US society. You should know how the lives of women changed during this period.

Key Topics

What were the 'Roaring Twenties'?

- In the aftermath of the First World War, Americans were determined to have a good time and increased prosperity meant there was more money to spend on entertainment. Young women were freer than ever before to behave as they liked – fashionable women who behaved scandously were known as 'flappers'. The popular image of the 1920s is that of one long party.
- The movie industry, based in Hollywood, developed rapidly. Stars like Charlie Chaplin, Rudolf Valentino and Mary Pickford

became household names. People worried about the impact of movies on public morality, and certainly the cinema portrayed and helped to create the greater social freedoms of the age. The Hays Office was set up in 1922 to try to enforce strict rules about what could be shown on screen. In 1927 the first 'talkie' was made – *The Jazz Singer*, starring Al Jolson.

- Sport became a form of mass entertainment. Huge crowds attended baseball games and boxing matches. Sports stars, like Babe Ruth, the baseball player, became popular heroes.

- There was a craze for new dances such as the Charleston and the Black Bottom. Jazz was the new form of music that emerged from earlier forms of black music like blues and ragtime. The great jazz players like Duke Ellington and Bessie Smith played at famous clubs such as the Cotton Club in Harlem, New York.

- During the 1920s sales of radios increased from $2 million a year to $600 million. The first national broadcasting network opened in 1926.

Summary Box 1

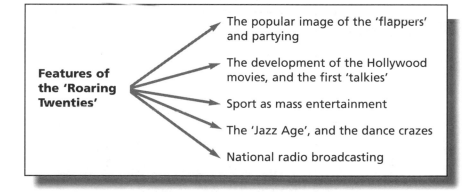

Features of the 'Roaring Twenties'
- The popular image of the 'flappers' and partying
- The development of the Hollywood movies, and the first 'talkies'
- Sport as mass entertainment
- The 'Jazz Age', and the dance crazes
- National radio broadcasting

How widespread was intolerance in US society?

- The First World War created anti-foreigner feeling. Many Americans worried about the amount of immigration that had created their 'melting-pot' society. The Johnson-Reid Act of 1924 put a limit on immigration of 150,000 people per year and stopped Asian immigration entirely.

- One of the worries about immigrants was that they might bring socialist ideas with them, which were seen as anti-capitalist and therefore anti-American. The government began to arrest and deport suspected socialist agitators, and a wave of anti-communist hysteria, known as the 'Red Scare', swept the country. This reached its peak when prominent politicians began to receive letter bombs and Attorney-General Palmer's house was blown up.

- The Sacco and Vanzetti case was a consequence of the 'Red Scare'. There was little evidence for the charge of murder which was brought against them, but they were immigrants and they were anarchist. Also, the public wanted a scapegoat for the wave of violence during the 'Red Scare'. They were found guilty and eventually executed, despite an international outcry.

- In the south, black people suffered under the 'Jim Crow' laws which kept them segregated from white people. Most black people lived in poverty and in permanent fear of lynch mobs. Discrimination was not quite as bad in the northern cities, but most black people there still had the poorest housing and found it hard to get decent jobs.
- The revival of the Ku Klux Klan in 1915 by William Simmons was evidence of extreme racism in US society. The Klan's hatred was not limited to black people; Catholics, Jews, foreigners, liberals and homosexuals were also targets. During the 1920s the Klan reached a peak of 5 million members.
- The Scopes Trial of 1925 illustrated the widening gulf that existed between the modern ideas of urban US society and the traditional, small-town beliefs of the country areas. Johnny Scopes was arrested for teaching Darwinism. The so-called 'Monkey Trial' which followed was a national sensation. Scopes was found guilty, but the anti-evolutionists lost the arguments against teaching evolution.

Summary Box 2

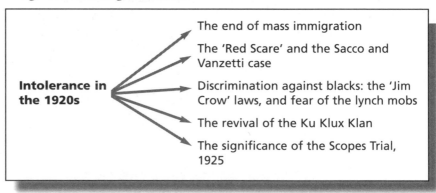

Intolerance in the 1920s
- The end of mass immigration
- The 'Red Scare' and the Sacco and Vanzetti case
- Discrimination against blacks: the 'Jim Crow' laws, and fear of the lynch mobs
- The revival of the Ku Klux Klan
- The significance of the Scopes Trial, 1925

Why was prohibition introduced and later repealed?

In 1919 the US Congress passed the 18th Amendment to the Constitution. This introduced prohibition on the sale, manufacture and transport of alcohol. The Volstead Act of 1920 gave the Federal government power to enforce prohibition. From January 1920, the US was officially 'dry'. Why had this happened?

1 Some states already had their own prohibition laws. The 18th Amendment simply made prohibition nationwide.
2 It was claimed that alcohol caused many social problems, like violence and immorality. If it were banned, it was claimed, the USA would become a better place.
3 Anti-alcohol pressure groups campaigned effectively for prohibition. The most famous was the Anti-Saloon League.
4 The First World War created strong anti-German feeling. Many of the USA's brewers were of German descent.

- However, prohibition had the undesired effect of making alcohol more attractive. Illegal bars, called 'speakeasies', opened all over the country and consumption of alcohol actually went up.

- Many people tried to make their own alcohol. This 'moonshine' could be lethal and some people died from its effects.
- It proved impossible to prevent alcohol being smuggled into the USA. Many smugglers made huge amounts from this illegal trade.
- Prohibition gave an enormous boost to crime. Gangsters organised the manufacture and sale of alcohol. From the huge profits they made they could bribe policemen and city officials. Violent feuding between gangs led to incidents like the St Valentine's Day Massacre of 1929 in Chicago, when Al Capone's gang murdered six members of the rival North Side gang.
- It soon became obvious that prohibition was a failure, but it took a long time before it came to an end. The Depression made a difference: it seemed crazy to spend public money on enforcing an unpopular law when, if alcohol were made legal again, it would create many jobs for the unemployed.
- When Roosevelt became President he took immediate steps to repeal prohibition. This was done by the passing of the 21st Amendment, and prohibition ended in December 1933.

Summary Box 3

Effects of prohibition

- Alcohol consumption increased and 'speakeasies' opened
- Production of illegal 'moonshine' and deaths from poisoning
- Smuggling by sea and across the Canadian border
- Crime wave with gangsters profiting from prohibition. Organised crime funded other types of criminal activity
- Corruption of police and public officials
- Failure of prohibition obvious, but repealed only in 1933

How far did the role of women change in the 1920s?

- The public image of women in the 1920s is the 'flapper' – the outrageous party girl. In reality, only a minority of women were like this.
- Women in the 1920s were more free. In 1920 they got the right to vote. More went out to work and became financially independent.
- Even the lives of women who stayed at home became easier. Contraception meant that they no longer had to have large families. Labour-saving devices like washing machines, refrigerators and vacuum cleaners made housework much less demanding.
- Many older women found the changes threatening and improper. They found the new fashions scandalous.

- The changes in women's behaviour were much more obvious in cities than in small towns. Away from the cities, traditional values and behaviour continued.

What do I Know?

1 Where was the centre of the US film industry?
2 Name one of the famous film stars of the 1920s.
3 What was the title of the first 'talkie'?
4 What was Babe Ruth famous for?
5 Where was the Cotton Club?
6 Name one of the dance crazes of the 1920s.
7 What limit did the Johnson-Reid Act of 1924 place on annual immigration?
8 Name the Attorney-General whose house was blown up at the height of the 'Red Scare'.
9 Who refounded the Ku Klux Klan in 1915?
10 Name one group other than blacks who were a target of Klan violence.
11 Who was put on trial in 1925 for teaching Darwinism?
12 What popular name was given to this trial?
13 Which act of 1920 gave the Federal Government power to enforce prohibition?
14 Who was responsible for the St Valentine's Day Massacre?
15 What were 'flappers'?

My score …

What was the importance of:

- the Hays Office
- the 'Red Scare'
- the 'Jim Crow' laws
- the Anti-Saloon League?

Exam Type Question

The Optional Depth Studies are tested in Section C of Paper 1. On your chosen Depth Study you will have to answer two questions. The first will be a compulsory source-based question. There will be three sources and three sub-questions to answer. The second question will be structured, also consisting of three parts (worth 4, 6 and 10 marks for each part). There will be two of these structured questions, and you choose one.

Here is an example of a structured question on the US society in the 1920s.

(a) What were the main features of the 'Roaring Twenties'?
(4 marks)

(b) Explain why Sacco and Vanzetti were executed. **(6 marks)**

(c) Here are three reasons why prohibition came to an end:
(i) the growth of crime;
(ii) the impact of the Depression;
(iii) the election of Roosevelt as president.

Was any one of these reasons more important than the others? Explain your answer. **(10 marks)**

Have a go yourself at parts (a) and (c) – here are a couple of students' answers to part (b).

Answer 1

Sacco and Vanzetti were executed because they were found guilty of murder. They were charged with robbing a shoe factory, and during the robbery they shot two people dead. They were anarchists and when they were arrested they had guns, so the police reckoned they had done it.

Answer 2

The legal reason why Sacco and Vanzetti were executed is that they were found guilty of murder. They were supposed to have shot two people during a raid on a shoe factory. However, the real reason is that their case occurred at the time of the Red Scare. Hysteria about foreigners and communists was at its height. They were both recent immigrants, and they were anarchists – for most people this was enough to prove they were guilty. Their trial was a farce, and there was an international campaign to save them, but Americans demanded a scapegoat for the outrages committed during the Red Scare.

Examiner's Comments: Answer 1

2 out of 6

This answer takes a rather narrow view of why Sacco and Vanzetti were executed. It doesn't look at all at the broader context of the case, and concentrates instead on the crime they were supposed to have committed. Nonetheless, the answer does identify a reason (found guilty of murder) and explains it.

Answer 2

6 out of 6

This answer is more satisfactory as the student realises that the real reasons Sacco and Vanzetti were executed had little to do with whether they were guilty of the crime. Using the context of the Red Scare and the hatred of foreigners which characterised the early 1920s is a much better approach to answering the question, but the narrowly legal issue of the crime is also covered. Both reasons and explanations for the reasons are given.

5.3 What were the causes and consequences of the Wall Street Crash?

Topic Summary

During the economic boom of the 1920s, investors got used to the idea that prices of shares would always go up. The Wall Street stock market in New York was like a giant bubble waiting to burst. One problem was that by the end of the 1920s there were clear signs that the US economy was slowing down. People began to worry that the boom had been built upon debt. On 'Black Thursday' (24 October 1929) prices of shares began to fall sharply. Within a few days, thousands of people had been bankrupted. But the Crash had only just started. Share prices continued to fall until 1932, by which time they had lost four-fifths of their value. The effects on the USA and on the world economy were profound. Bankruptcies led to unemployment, which led to falling production and economic disaster. By 1932, 12 million Americans were out of work. President Hoover, a Republican, believed governments should not interfere in business. He thought the Depression would solve itself. When it didn't he tried some small-scale schemes to create jobs, but they made no difference. All over the country there were homeless and destitute people, desperate for work. They were finally given some hope in the presidential election of 1932 when Franklin D. Roosevelt was the Democrats' candidate against Hoover. Roosevelt promised a 'New Deal' for the US people, and he won a landslide victory.

What do I Need to Know?

You will need to understand the causes of the Wall Street Crash of October 1929 and, in particular, the role that speculation played in the collapse of the stock market. You should understand why the fall in share prices was so damaging for the US economy as a whole, and how the Crash led to the Great Depression. You will need to know about the social consequences of the Crash, and how politicians tried to deal with the effects of mass unemployment. You should be able to explain the issues which divided the candidates in the 1932 presidential election, and analyse why Roosevelt won.

Key Topics

How far was speculation responsible for the Wall Street Crash?

- During the 1920s the Wall Street stock market shared in the economic boom. Prices of shares rose sharply (shares are a stake in a real business). People got used to the idea that share prices would always go up, which encouraged speculation. $100 invested in shares in 1920 would have been worth around $325 by 1929.

142

- People borrowed money to buy shares. They were allowed to buy 'on the margin' – paying only a small percentage of the shares' real price, then reselling at a profit before having to pay the balance. Banks were happy to lend money to speculators.
- However, everything depended on the price of shares going up. If they went down, people would lose the stake and end up owing money.
- By the end of the 1920s, the US economy was slowing down. Demand for consumer goods was falling, tariffs on international trade made it hard to export, and the burden of hire-purchase debt was becoming a worry.
- Confidence in the US economy was starting to decline. Share prices began to fall.

Summary Box 1

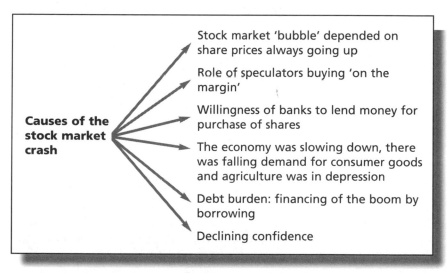

Causes of the stock market crash

Stock market 'bubble' depended on share prices always going up

Role of speculators buying 'on the margin'

Willingness of banks to lend money for purchase of shares

The economy was slowing down, there was falling demand for consumer goods and agriculture was in depression

Debt burden: financing of the boom by borrowing

Declining confidence

What impact did the Wall Street Crash have on the economy?

- On 'Black Thursday' (24 October 1929) the fall in share prices turned into panic. Prices plunged, and desperate investors sold their shares to try to cut their losses. Thousands were bankrupted. But Black Thursday was only the beginning. On the worst day of the Crash the value of shares fell by £10,000 million. The stock market went into free fall and didn't stop falling for three years. By 1932 share prices on average were one-fifth of what they had been in 1929.
- The stock market crash was an economic disaster. Thousands of people lost everything, and firms and banks went bust. Unemployment rose sharply, eventually peaking at nearly 13 million in 1933. Production fell, as people had less to spend on goods, and falling production meant more unemployment. In 1929, 4.5 million cars were sold; only 1 million were sold in 1932. The economy was in a downward spiral.
- By 1933 the economy was producing only 20 per cent of what it had in 1929.

- President Hoover believed that the economy would eventually recover by itself. Like all Republicans, he didn't think governments should get involved in the economy. He took some half-hearted measures, like asking employers not to sack workers, and giving loans to businesses in trouble, but they were not significant enough to make a difference. In 1930 he made matters worse by agreeing the Hawley-Smoot tariff, which placed even higher tariffs on imports. This inevitably led to retaliation by other countries through a reduction in US export trade.
- Hoover's name became associated with the effects of the Depression. Shanty towns built by the homeless unemployed were called 'Hoovervilles' and the newspapers the destitute used to cover themselves at night were known as 'Hoover blankets'.

What were the social consequences of the Wall Street Crash?

- The USA was not a welfare state, so those made unemployed faced ruin. Families lost their homes, or were split up when the father left to search for work.
- The unemployed relied on charity. Queues of unemployed waiting in line for food became a common sight. Many cities ran emergency relief schemes, but by 1932 money for these was running out.
- The homeless built shanty towns of scrap metal and tents.
- The government lost support through its treatment of the Bonus Marchers in the summer of 1932. The Bonus Marchers were homeless veterans of the armed forces who had been promised a payment for war service. They wanted early payment of the bonus, but their camps in Washington were forcibly destroyed by soldiers.

Summary Box 2

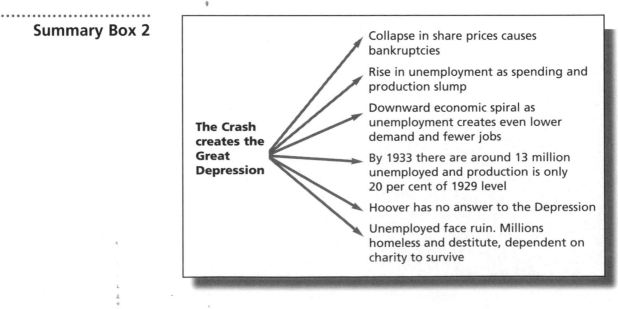

The Crash creates the Great Depression

- Collapse in share prices causes bankruptcies
- Rise in unemployment as spending and production slump
- Downward economic spiral as unemployment creates even lower demand and fewer jobs
- By 1933 there are around 13 million unemployed and production is only 20 per cent of 1929 level
- Hoover has no answer to the Depression
- Unemployed face ruin. Millions homeless and destitute, dependent on charity to survive

Why did Roosevelt win the presidential election of 1932?

- The Democrats' candidate in the 1932 election was Franklin D. Roosevelt. He came from a wealthy family from New York State, but had been crippled by polio.
- As Governor of New York from 1928, Roosevelt had made a reputation for helping the state's unemployed by using public money to fund job-creation schemes.
- The Republican candidate was President Hoover. Everyone knew what Hoover stood for. He had failed to deal with the Depression and he was unpopular.
- It wasn't entirely clear what Roosevelt stood for, although he promised a 'New Deal' for the US people. What impressed people about Roosevelt, though, was his energy and determination to do *something*. He seemed to offer optimism and hope.
- In the presidential election of 1932, Roosevelt won a landslide victory. He was chosen by 42 of the 48 states.

What do I Know?

1   Where is Wall Street?

2   By 1929, approximately how much would $100 invested in shares in 1920 have been worth?

3   Give one sign of the economic slowdown the US economy was experiencing by the late 1920s.

4   What name was given to the first day of the stock market crash?

5   By how much did the value of shares fall on the worst day of the crash?

6   What was the decline in the numbers of cars sold in the USA between 1929 and 1932?

7   How many people were unemployed by 1933?

8   What political party did Hoover belong to?

9   What was one of the measures Hoover took to try to deal with the Depression?

10   What were 'Hoovervilles'?

11   Where did the Bonus Marchers demonstrate in 1932?

12   From what physical disability did Roosevelt suffer?

13   What post did Roosevelt hold when he became the Democrats' presidential candidate in 1932?

14   What promise did Roosevelt make to the US people in his acceptance speech when he was chosen as the Democrats' candidate?

15   How many of the 48 states of the USA chose Roosevelt in the 1932 presidential election?

My score ...

What was the importance of:
- buying 'on the margin'
- 'Black Thursday'
- the Hawley-Smoot tariff
- the Bonus Marchers?

The Optional Depth Studies are tested in Section C of Paper 1. On your chosen Depth Study you will have to answer two questions. The first will be a compulsory source-based question. There will be three sources and three sub-questions to answer. The second question will be structured, also consisting of three parts (worth 4, 6 and 10 marks for each part). There will be two of these structured questions, and you choose one.

Here is an example of a structured question on US society in the 1920s.

(a) What were the social consequences of the Wall Street Crash? **(4 marks)**

(b) Explain why the Wall Street Crash happened in October 1929. **(6 marks)**

(c) 'The most important reason Roosevelt was elected President in 1932 was that he offered a "New Deal" to the US people.' Do you agree with this statement? Explain your answer. **(10 marks)**

Have a go yourself at parts (a) and (b) – here are a couple of students' answers to part (c).

Answer 1

No, this was not the most important reason. The most important reason was that Hoover did not have a clue what to do and was useless, so the US people would have chosen anyone to get rid of him.

Answer 2

There were reasons for choosing Roosevelt, and there were reasons for not choosing Hoover. Roosevelt seemed to offer people hope. It wasn't clear what his New Deal would be, but at least he was promising to do something. People knew from his record as Governor of New York that he was willing to use public money to help the unemployed. In contrast, people no longer had any faith in Hoover. They knew he would not take strong action to end the Depression. He had had plenty of chances in the previous three years, and he hadn't achieved anything, so why would he now? In addition, his treatment of the Bonus Marchers had made him look heartless and uncaring, so by 1932 he was pretty unpopular.

**Examiner's
Comments:
Answer 1**

3 out of 10
Not the most detailed answer, but it makes a point. Although there is no specific historical knowledge shown, the writer has a general awareness that Hoover had failed and that his unpopularity would make any alternative candidate look a better bet. For suggesting a single alternative reason and explaining it (as this answer does), you could get up to 5 marks. However, this is a very weak example.

Answer 2

7 out of 10
This shows a good level of knowledge and it looks at both sides by explaining why Roosevelt was an attractive candidate, and why Hoover was not. However, it falls short of being a top-level answer because it does not properly address the question of which reason was the *most important*. The student has not made a comparison of the different factors given. The very best answers would not only *compare* the factors, but would also reach a balanced *conclusion* showing how the factors relate to each other. Here, for example, Roosevelt would not have been offering a 'New Deal' if Hoover had not already failed to cope with the effects of the Depression.

5.4 How successful was the New Deal?

Roosevelt was determined to use the powers of the government to tackle the Depression. In his first 'Hundred Days' in office a whole series of new measures was introduced to deal with the banking crisis, to help farmers, to make work for the unemployed, to assist industry and to revive depressed areas. Government organisations, known as the 'alphabet agencies', were set up to implement the 'New Deal' legislation. In the first phase of the New Deal, up to 1935, the government took a far greater role in the running of the economy than ever before. This produced opposition from the rich and from businessmen, who saw Roosevelt's measures as a form of socialism. Several New Deal laws were declared unconstitutional by the Supreme Court. Roosevelt tried to intimidate the Court by threatening to appoint six new judges, but this caused such an outcry that he backed down. Other critics of the New Deal claimed it did not go far enough in protecting the interests of the poor and achieving social justice. There has been much debate about how effective the New Deal was. Unemployment fell, but did not disappear, and in 1937–8 the USA was hit by a renewed wave of unemployment. Only after the onset of war in 1939 did the USA's factories really get back to work again.

What do I Need to Know?

You will need to know about the main New Deal measures introduced by Roosevelt in 1933, and have an awareness of the extent to which the New Deal changed or had to be modified in the ensuing years. You will need to understand why not all Americans approved of the New Deal, and to know what criticisms were made of it. In particular you will need to know about Roosevelt's confrontation with the Supreme Court, and how it was resolved. You should know how far Roosevelt was able to solve the problem of unemployment, and be able to judge the extent to which the New Deal was a success.

Key Topics

What was the New Deal of 1933?

- The day of Roosevelt's inauguration as President, he faced a banking crisis. His Emergency Banking Act forced the banks to stay closed for four days. Then Roosevelt permanently shut down the weakest banks and, in a broadcast to the nation, he appealed for calm, urging people to leave their money in the banks. It worked and the banking system was saved from collapse. In 1934, he set up the Securities and Exchange Commission to control the activities of the Stock Market.

- Roosevelt's first 'Hundred Days' as President saw dozens of emergency measures passed. He started his 'fireside chats' – radio broadcasts when he would speak directly to the nation, explaining his policies as if he were chatting to friends.
- The Agricultural Adjustment Act helped farmers by destroying surplus production and compensating them for the loss, and the Agricultural Adjustment Administration (AAA) was set up to put the Act into operation. In this way prices could rise, and farming would recover.
- The unemployed were helped. The Federal Emergency Relief Administration (FERA) gave government grants to local government to provide emergency help for the destitute. The Civilian Conservation Corps (CCC) created jobs for young men in useful environmental work.
- The National Industrial Recovery Act set up two important agencies: the National Recovery Administration (NRA) negotiated with industry to establish agreements on pay and working conditions, and the Public Works Administration (PWA) used unemployed skilled workers on public construction projects.
- The Home Owners' Loan Corporation (HOLC) gave loans to the temporarily unemployed to prevent them losing their homes to the banks.
- The Tennessee Valley was a particularly depressed area. The Tennessee Valley Authority (TVA) was set up to regenerate the area by constructing dams which would provide electricity and encourage industry to develop.
- The agencies set up by the government to administer the New Deal were, for the obvious reason, called 'alphabet agencies'.
- The 21st Amendment to the Constitution, passed in 1933, brought prohibition to an end.

Summary Box 1

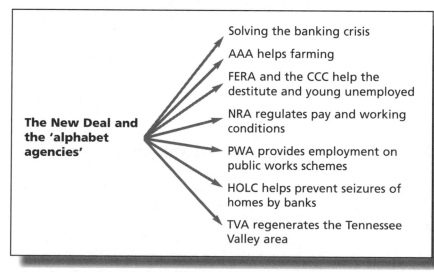

The New Deal and the 'alphabet agencies'

- Solving the banking crisis
- AAA helps farming
- FERA and the CCC help the destitute and young unemployed
- NRA regulates pay and working conditions
- PWA provides employment on public works schemes
- HOLC helps prevent seizures of homes by banks
- TVA regenerates the Tennessee Valley area

How far did the New Deal change after 1935?

- The first burst of New Deal legislation was aimed at resolving the immediate economic crisis and its effects. By 1935 the situation was changing.

- Roosevelt faced a re-election campaign in 1936. His critics had become more vocal, both on the right where business was complaining about government controls and on the left where the criticism was that Roosevelt was not doing enough for the poor. Perhaps most ominously, the Supreme Court had begun to declare some of the New Deal legislation unconstitutional.

The Second New Deal

During 1935 Roosevelt introduced another phase of reforms which has been called the 'Second New Deal'. This focused more on establishing improved welfare and labour rights:

- The Social Security Act (1935) set up a national insurance scheme which provided old age pensions, unemployment benefits and support for handicapped people.
- The Wagner Act (1935) confirmed the right of workers to join trade unions.
- The Works Progress Administration (WPA) was set up to coordinate government efforts to find work for the unemployed. Because of its emphasis on finding work that was socially useful, it not only funded construction projects, but also employed out-of-work artists, writers and photographers in community art projects.

Summary Box 2

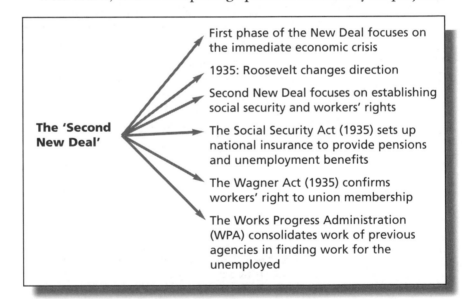

The 'Second New Deal'

- First phase of the New Deal focuses on the immediate economic crisis
- 1935: Roosevelt changes direction
- Second New Deal focuses on establishing social security and workers' rights
- The Social Security Act (1935) sets up national insurance to provide pensions and unemployment benefits
- The Wagner Act (1935) confirms workers' right to union membership
- The Works Progress Administration (WPA) consolidates work of previous agencies in finding work for the unemployed

Why did the New Deal encounter opposition?

- The most obvious opponents of the New Deal were the rich and businessmen who resented the government's interference in the economy. They thought the New Deal was a form of socialism, and was un-American.
- A majority of judges in the Supreme Court disapproved of the New Deal. One by one they declared New Deal laws, like the National Industrial Recovery Act and the Agricultural Adjustment Act, unconstitutional. Roosevelt feared that the whole New Deal would be dismantled by the judges, so he

threatened to enlarge the court to 15 judges. This would have enabled him to appoint six of his own supporters, but it caused an outcry as it made him look like a dictator. Eventually he backed down, realising that Congress would never approve of his plan.

- Radical critics like Father Coughlin (the 'Radio Priest') and Francis Townsend complained that the New Deal did not go far enough in helping the USA's poor. Townsend campaigned for pension reform through his 'Townsend Clubs'. They claimed that Roosevelt was more interested in preserving society, rather than changing it. Roosevelt's most dangerous critic was Huey Long, the disreputable but popular Governor of Louisiana. With his 'Share Our Wealth' scheme, Long promised to confiscate the wealth of millionaires and redistribute the money so that every American would have a home, a car and a radio. Long was assassinated in 1935, but might otherwise have challenged Roosevelt in the 1936 election. As it was, Roosevelt easily beat Alf Landon, his Republican opponent, to be re-elected in 1936.

Summary Box 3

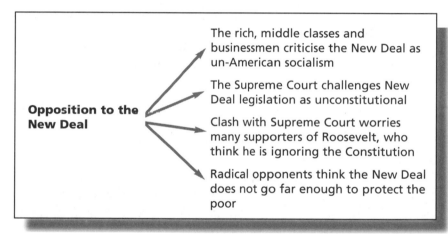

Opposition to the New Deal

The rich, middle classes and businessmen criticise the New Deal as un-American socialism

The Supreme Court challenges New Deal legislation as unconstitutional

Clash with Supreme Court worries many supporters of Roosevelt, who think he is ignoring the Constitution

Radical opponents think the New Deal does not go far enough to protect the poor

Why did unemployment persist despite the New Deal?

- The New Deal found work for millions of unemployed Americans, but it did not actually solve the problem. Critics said the new jobs were not 'real' – if the government withdrew its money, the jobs would disappear.
- Many employers remained deeply hostile to workers' rights, and tried to smash trade unions which recruited their employees.
- The New Deal did much to help farmers, but there were agricultural problems which could not be solved. Drought in the prairie states turned many areas into 'dustbowls'. Farmers and their families were forced off the land, and many of these poor 'Okies' migrated to California to look for work.
- The New Deal did nothing specifically to help black people, who constituted the single largest group in poverty. Roosevelt's reluctance to alienate his supporters amongst southern Democrats meant that he did nothing to address race issues.

- In 1937, under the mistaken impression that the economy was recovering, Roosevelt cut back government spending. The economy immediately slumped, and unemployment rose again.

Was the New Deal a failure?

- Judgements on the New Deal vary. The unemployment problem was solved by the Second World War, not by Roosevelt. Nonetheless, Roosevelt reduced unemployment in the New Deal. Work was provided for millions of people.
- Critics of the New Deal focus on the far wider role for government that Roosevelt created. They criticise the bureaucracy and inefficiency of government intervention, arguing that free enterprise is better at running industries than governments.
- Roosevelt's real achievement was to give hope back to the USA. His open, optimistic personality was ideal for coping with the challenges of the Depression.

What do I Know?

1 What did the Emergency Banking Act of 1933 force the banks to do?

2 Which organisation was set up in 1934 to control the activities of the stock market?

3 What did the letters CCC stand for?

4 Which two agencies were set up by the National Industrial Recovery Act?

5 What was the job of the Home Owners' Loan Corporation?

6 How did the TVA plan to control the Tennessee River and benefit the people of the area at the same time?

7 What did the 21st Amendment to the Constitution bring to an end?

8 Name a New Deal law that was declared unconstitutional by the Supreme Court.

9 What did the Wagner Act give to workers?

10 Who was Roosevelt's opponent in the 1936 presidential election?

11 How many new judges did Roosevelt want to appoint to the Supreme Court, and how many judges in total would there then have been?

12 Name the radical critic of Roosevelt who was known as the 'radio priest'.

13 Which critic of Roosevelt was Governor of Louisiana?

14 What did the 'Townsend Clubs' aim to achieve?

15 What was the 'dustbowl'?

My score ...

What was the importance of:

- the Agricultural Adjustment Administration
- the National Recovery Administration
- the 'fireside chats'
- Huey Long?

Exam Type Question

Thc Optional Depth Studies are tested in Section C of Paper 1. On your chosen Depth Study you will have to answer two questions. The first will be a compulsory source-based question. There will be three sources and three sub-questions to answer. The source-based question carries 20 marks in total, with the three parts each being worth 6, 7 and 7 marks, though not necessarily in that order. Although the questions are source-based and test source-handling skills, they also require you to use your knowledge.

The second question will be structured, also consisting of three parts (worth 4, 6 and 10 marks for each part). There will be two of these structured questions, and you choose one.

Take a look at the following source-based example. Study the sources carefully, and then answer the questions which follow.

Source A

▲ A British cartoon of 1935 commenting on the Supreme Court's decision to rule the NRA illegal.

Source B

America is in peril. For three long years the New Deal administration has dishonoured American traditions and flagrantly betrayed the pledges on which the Democratic Party sought and received public support. The rights and liberties of American citizens have been violated. It has bred fear and hesitation in commerce and industry thus prolonging the Depression. It has destroyed the morale of many of our people and made them dependent upon government.

▲ An extract from the Republican Party's manifesto for the 1936 presidential election.

Source C

▲ **An American cartoon published in 1936 shows the reaction of businessmen to the New Deal.**

(a) Study Source A.
Do you think this cartoon was drawn by a supporter or by an opponent of Roosevelt? Use the source and your knowledge to explain your answer. **(6 marks)**

(b) Study Source B.
Do you think this manifesto would have made people want to vote for the Republicans? Use the source and your own knowledge to explain your answer. **(7 marks)**

(c) Study Source C.
Why do you think this cartoon was published in 1936? Use the source and your knowledge to explain your answer. **(7 marks)**

Have a go yourself at parts (b) and (c) – here are a couple of students' answers to part (a).

Answer 1

I would say that the cartoon was drawn by an opponent because Roosevelt is shown as a violent person who is trying to drown the man. He wants to push the man down into the sea which is the Depression. It shows Roosevelt was a bad person and a supporter would never show him like this.

Answer 2

> This cartoon isn't criticising Roosevelt. The people the cartoonist thinks are to blame are the judges of the Supreme Court. So, it must be done by a supporter who thinks that the Supreme Court judges are going to let the USA drown in the Depression by banning all the New Deal laws. The 'illegal act' is the National Recovery Administration (you can see it mentioned on the boat) which the Court had declared unconstitutional. The artist is being ironic because an illegal act would be to drown someone, so this cartoon is criticising the Supreme Court for wanting to push the USA back into depression. This is why I think the cartoon was drawn by a supporter of Roosevelt.

Examiner's Comments: Answer 1

1 out of 6

Cartoons often cause problems of interpretation. Weaker students can very easily be misled by what cartoons *appear* to show, particularly where the cartoonist uses irony or sarcasm to make a point, as in this example. The student has given a face-value judgement, which is, of course, a total misinterpretation. The answer is nonsense if judged alongside factual knowledge – why on earth would Roosevelt want to push the USA into depression? His New Deal was a plan to try to alleviate the Depression.

Answer 2

6 out of 6

This answer shows the difference that some contextual knowledge can make. The writer is aware of the attitude of the Supreme Court towards the New Deal and so sees that the cartoonist is on Roosevelt's side. The irony in the cartoonist's use of the phrase 'the illegal act' is brought out well, and the question's requirement to use background knowledge is met by the writer's reference to the Court's declaration of the National Recovery Administration as unconstitutional. This is an excellent answer which fully explains why the cartoon must have been drawn by a supporter of Roosevelt.